747

Matthew Boulton College Library

Classification no. 747

This book must be returned by the latest date stamped
below. To renew, telephone 0121 446 4545 ext 3169.
Fines will be charged on books returned late.

11. MAR
11. APR 02

02 MAY

08. OCT 02

05. NOV 02

28. APR 03

15 DEC 05
26 April

Dream interiors

HAZAR
P·U·B·L·I·S·H·I·N·G

Dream interiors

HAZAR
P·U·B·L·I·S·H·I·N·G

Author

Franc sco Asensio Cerver

Editorial manager

Paco Asensio

Design and layout

VERSUS

Text

Richard Rees

Elaine Fradley

Proofreading

Elaine Fradley

Photographers

Eugèni Pons
Jordi Miralles
Imanol Sistiaga
Chris Gascoigne

This edition published 1999 by Hazar Publishing Limited
147 Chiswick High Road, London, W4 2DT

First published in 1998
by Arco Editorial S.A.

© Copyright 1998 Francisco Asensio Cerver

Printed and bound in Spain

A catalogue record for this title is available from the British Library

ISBN: 1 847371 48 2

Contents

introduction	6
Present and past	16
Simple styling	18
An amalgam of elements	22
Open spaces	26
Secluded corners	28
Warm wood	30
Attention to detail	34
A temple of peace	36
Urban landscapes	38
Dazzling white	40
Highly personal	42
Living spaces	44
The mediterranean spirit	46
A summer house	48
Top of the hill	50
A rustic flavour	52
Power to the imagination	54
Reflections in glass	56
Making full use of the space	58
Overlooking the sea	60
A trio of aces	66
An interior full of life	68
Living in a warehouse	70
White on white	72
Sobriety and colour	76
Adapting to the environment	78
The search for balance	80
Open to the exterior	84
A maritime character	86
Simple elegance	88
Family life	90
A cheerful awakening	92
Around the fireplace	94
Upstairs downstairs	96
Welcoming ambiences	100
In a belvedere	104
Two original offices	108
Youthful freshness	110
Colour and fantasy	112
Everything is possible	114
An informal meeting	116
Daring elegance	118
Similar though different	122
A perfect layout	124
Recovering the past	126
Beneath the waves	128
Two very up-to-date kitchens	132
Waking up to a patio	136
Visual continuity	138
Warm orange	140
Changing levels	142
Unusual structures	146
Contained passion	148
Empty space	152
An art nouveau palace	154
Serene reality	158
Making the most of corners	160
Living in the city	162
Good ideas	166
In pink and blue	170
Well defined	172
A vital decor	174
Minimal expression	178
Brought up to date	180
The house of the future	184
The heart of the house	188
The plant kingdom	190
A fairy tale	192
A summer dining area	194
Country style brought up to date	196
A peaceful refuge	198
Touches of colour	200
Zone of passage	202
Experimental decoration	204

Intro

A well-designed interior is not just about the latest fashion or trend in interior design, it should also mirror the personality of the owner, reflecting habits and manias, interests and tastes. It finds nourishment in memories and experiences and should grow and develop, adapting to the passage of time and to new needs.

introduction

Some rooms speak of quiet, family-loving individuals; others of practical, dynamic people, lovers of social and urban life; and still others of sensitive, romantic characters who love to daydream. But homes are not just for show; they are used on a day-to-day basis, so it is vitally important that the decor should be faithful to its owner, to expectations and dreams, and to a personal way of looking at the world.

This book is meant to be a model and a source of inspiration for all those who would like to decorate their house. It provides ideas and suggests a number of interesting decorative resources. It presents present-day trends in interior decorating from all over the world, from the most traditional to the most innovative, and offers the reader a wide selection of interiors that, for one reason or another and regardless of style, are truly captivating.

The next few pages briefly describe the different themes to be found in the book.

Layout

Planning the space has to be the starting point in the design of any interior. This means not only how the individual pieces of furniture will fit into the space, but how the spaces relate to one another and how the circulation between them will work. Some of the interiors featured here are dual purpose, others fulfill one function only. Some are totally open plan; others are arranged in enclosed rooms. Some interiors are crammed with an abundance of decorative features and furniture, other interiors are more frugal and restrained, leaving considerable amounts of space free. Although it has not been possible to include plans of each area, in most cases the photographs show how successful the spatial planning has been and how the finished room works in use.

Materials

Different building materials each have their own particular character, but it can be quite possible to use them against this very successfully. Thus, natural stone, terracotta, wood and wrought iron may be thought of as rustic, but can equally well be used in a modern interior if it is done in the right way. In the same way, pale wood, concrete, lacquers, ceramics and parquet can be either modern, rustic or avant-garde, as can stainless steel, acid-treated glass and exposed brick. There are also the various possible textures of each material to consider.

Colours

The interiors featured in these pages cover the whole colour spectrum, from simple areas in pure white, through rooms in a limited palette, to those that are an explosion of colour in which vivid red is set against electric blue. Here colour is used to cater for all tastes and moods and one can get a very clear idea of which colours work well together and how certain effects might be achieved.

Decorative Styles

A wide range of decorative styles is featured, since nowadays almost anything goes. Here are modern interiors, easy to understand and rapidly accepted; rustic houses of a timeless, country-style beauty; romantic rooms, soft and almost feminine; hard and metallic, industrial, masculine environments; urban corners for uncompromising city-lovers; youthful, refreshing Mediterranean marine environments; interiors in period style; avant-garde rooms and loving restoration of exuberant art nouveau.

Balance and Rhythm

Rhythm and balance are two most important factors that must be considered during the design stages, since they can be largely responsible for the overall verdict on the end result. Balance can be achieved in many ways: by planning seating in a certain layout; by placing ornamental objects in one way or another; by either seeking perfect symmetry or deliberately disrupting it. The repetition of colours, spaces or features can create a rhythm that, occasionally and in order to add dynamism, may be brusquely interrupted.

Luxury and Austerity

Interiors may be simple and restrained, discreet and modest, shunning excess and ostentation and at odds with overwhelming luxury. In these cases natural elements are often used, extracted from the earth, reminding us of our origins and speaking of Nature. There are times, however, when just the opposite is required, when wealth can be openly displayed. Then an abundance of sophisticated furniture, large paintings, pieces of incalculable value, Roman busts, classical sculptures, walls decorated with highly elaborate frescoes, gilt details, bold borders — all work together to create a rich ambience and a highly personal universe in which nothing is superfluous.

Textiles

Practical, youthful, fresh textiles predominate in these interiors. Blinds are used in preference to classic curtains in most cases. Plain carpets, rich Oriental rugs, textured upholstery, white linen, voiles and lace - all add their individual note to the finished rooms.

Textiles are often used purely for their texture, but carpets, cushions and bedspreads are occasionally called upon to provide touches of colour in otherwise monochrome environments.

Lighting

Most of the photographs show interiors that open onto the exterior through huge glazed doors or windows. Light floods in, all-pervading and emphasizing the beauty of colours and textures. Sometimes this natural light is controlled with curtains or blinds, creating an interplay of light and shadow.

Artificial light enters the scene either directly, in the form of spotlights or small, strategically placed lamps to highlight a particular feature, or indirectly via carefully concealed sources.

Furniture

The dominant trend in furnishing seems to be a mixture of several styles: classic, rustic, modern, avant-garde. In this way, an antique desk, an Elizabethan chest of drawers or a classic easy chair take can its place beside a selection of modern pieces.

There is also an abundance of modular or made-to-measure furniture, pieces that adapt masterfully to the characteristics and irregularities of the spaces that house them. Metallic industrial structures are still used in the right interior, while seating tends towards spacious sofas with large cushions.

Decorative Accessories

Although accessories are not always given their due importance, their presence helps to achieve a certain rhythm, to establish an ambience or define the owners' personality.

Pictures always add to an interior and can also be hung creatively to achieve different decorative effects. When arranged geometrically they provide order and classicism, marking a steady, traditional rhythm; if they are arranged in asymmetrical or irregular groups they create an impression of deliberate chaos, highly appropriate for youthful, informal rooms.

Plants provide freshness and vitality, and are sometimes used to hide awkward corners or to establish balance. Small items, such as cushions, vases or throws tend to be used as visual counterpoints or to introduce flashes of colour to break up monochrome schemes. Mementoes of experiences and special moments add personality to the room and are often made into major features, or even have the entire interior scheme based upon them.

Living rooms and Dining rooms

This book shows a variety of living rooms and dining rooms in all styles and for all possible tastes. Classic, rustic, postmodern, up-to-date and youthful, casual and practical decors; white, neutral or colourful; suitable for urban spaces, country or beach houses. There are also a great number of different dining, coffee and occasional tables, as well as many other furniture items featured within these rooms. There are so many ideas on offer that it would be very hard not to find one that would please the most discerning tastes.

Kitchens

The kitchen offers a wide range of possibilities: classic white-tiled kitchens combined with rustic furniture; industrial-style kitchens, cold and metallic; cheerful, colourful kitchens, characterized by a naïve charm; kitchens either independent or part of the whole living-dining room area.

Bedrooms

A bedroom is not just a place to sleep; it should also be a place to relax in, to prepare for the day ahead or wind down from the day just past. It is a very personal area, lending itself to strong statements about the owner. Many of the bedrooms featured provide the key to an understanding of the rest of the decor: romantic or rustic, minimalist or crowded — bedrooms whose aesthetics might be similar to, or completely different from, that of the rest of the house. Large bedrooms can also perform a dual function, with personal study area, or an ensuite bathroom.

Bathrooms

Bathrooms are the most private, personal rooms in the whole house, usually retreating behind conventional walls and doors. In a few of the interiors featured in these pages the bathroom is more public, being either open to the bedroom or only separated from more social areas by a light structure. In the design of these rooms, lighting is vital. They often have no natural light, so artificial lighting has to be both functional and beautiful.

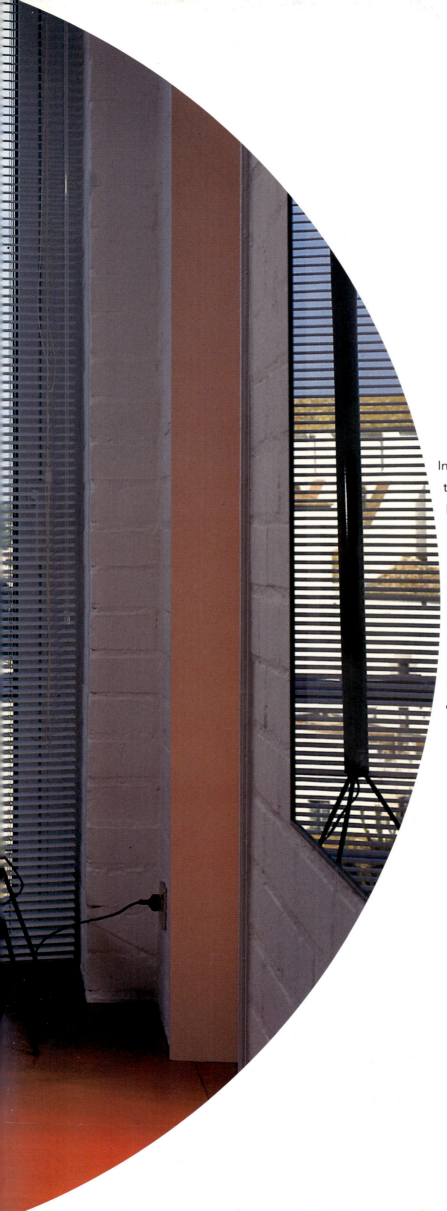

Interior design and decoration is an art, a complex art that is difficult to define. To stringently follow its rules and establish a perfect and harmonious balance; to arrange all the different elements with a calculated symmetry and choose furniture of beautiful design and high quality; to paint the walls in fashionable colours and cover the floor with the best materials — all this is not enough. Something will still be missing: life.

When decorating a home it is important to first look around and compare styles and trends, but this is not enough. It must also be faithful to its owner's personality and have something of significance in each room. Only in this way is it possible to create a house with its own soul.

Present and past

These two bedrooms are radically different. One has a great deal of period charm and could have been created at least a century ago. The other, in contrast, is modern, youthful and very simple. Both, in their own way, are equally charming and distinctive.

The period bedroom uses the beauty of a plain farmhouse interior, with its bare wooden beams, simple white walls and sturdy polished doors. The effect is enhanced by the sober, austere bedside tables, an old sewing machine transformed into a console table and, above all, the exquisitely romantic wrought-iron bed with its linen sheets.

Similar elements are used in the second bedroom, but the effect is quite different: the ambience continues to be romantic, but the style is much more modern. The rustic wrought-iron bed has been replaced by a contemporary version of a four-poster, with an elegant canopy. The antiques have been replaced by more avant-garde furniture. The walls are a vivid

electric blue, the sharp coldness of this colour softened by the warm, rich glow of polished wood. As in the previous case, the ceiling beams have been left bare.

These two bedrooms show us different ways of evoking a single image. While the first is a literal reproduction of the decor and ambience of a period bedroom, the second uses the same elements in a very abstract and even simple way to create a present-day reworking of the theme.

As the beauty of these two examples shows, a successful decor is not based on using any one particular style. Each of these two interiors possesses its own charm, its own character, its 'raison d'être'.

The wrought-iron bed is the main feature in this period bedroom.

The rich blue of the walls gives this bedroom its character.

Simple
styling

Fresh and luminous, the ambience of this home is based on simplicity; it may be for this reason that the atmosphere created transmits a special feeling of serenity, able to ease even the most troubled mind.

In many ways the interior seems to be a continuation of the exterior, since the terracotta flooring is used throughout and the large picture windows provide clear views of the garden, which can be enjoyed without leaving the house. The large expanse of glass also allows natural light to flow in freely, so the space seems very open and airy.

The key area in this house is this living-dining room, in which all family activity takes place. It is dominated by a dramatic modern fireplace with an open canopy and flue. Set in front of this, the main seating consists of two low, comfortable, garnet-red sofas set around a natural sisal rug. The coffee table is simple in design, with firm, straight lines.

The dining area has an elegant, modern, rectangular table, with an acid-etched glass top and stylized legs, and a set of contemporary chairs. Behind the dining area, a cantilevered staircase leads to the floor above.

The living room is dominated by the stark lines of a very modern fireplace.

The terracotta floor and leafy plants make the interior seem like an extension of the exterior.

Using a simple finish in elements like the fireplace and the staircase produces an almost sculptural effect, rather like works of art displayed against the plain white walls of a gallery.

The staircase in particular is suggestive of a great backbone sweeping up into the area above. Each step recalls a vertebra, in a metaphor that highlights the importance of this architectural element within the life of the house.

The bedroom echoes the simple and youthful style of the living-dining room. The walls are painted a clear, pale yellow: a relaxing colour that creates a feeling of spaciousness.

Good taste is often based on simplicity and restraint, and the bedroom is a good example of this. In such an uncluttered room, the selection and placing of pieces of furniture takes on a major significance. The small trunk pressed into service as a

bedside table becomes a focal point in the room in the absence of other furniture and decorative elements.

Each individual element comes into its own in relation to its immediate context, and many of the best organized spaces in this house revolve around contrast. The significant elements are carefully isolated; what better way to highlight an item than to place it in an incongruous setting?

Simplicity, natural materials and plain neutral colours cre the main characteristics of this interior.

An uncluttered, relaxing atmosphere has been created for the bedroom.

An amalgam of elements

Nobody could remain indifferent to this eclectic interior: on every side and in every corner there are curious pieces and unusual features just waiting to be discovered by the curious eye of the visitor.

The mixture of elements and styles is the key to this kind of decor, into which almost anything will fit. Smooth white walls offset the deliberate crudeness of highly original frescoes, while at the same time several small partitions set at various angles break up what would otherwise be the rather monotonous symmetry of the room. On the ceiling, the wooden beams add a touch of tradition. The floor is of parquet, inset with areas of mosaic; the different materials are used to separate spaces.

This interior consists of two rectangular rooms. The larger of the two is the living room, in which the latest designs combine with exotic or ethnic furniture. Next to the

At first glance, the areas of mosaic in the floor look like highly patterned rugs. In the foreground is a curious piece of furniture design.

The eclectic mixture of elements that characterizes this interior creates a rich visual feast.

living room is the library, with its books stored on several light, modular elements. The second room acts as a study, and the furniture has been chosen to reinterpret the style typical of offices. In this context, the elegant grand piano is an item that both disorientates and seduces.

One of the greatest merits of this room is the way that the partitions and the floor are used both to create a highly unusual subdivision of the area, and at the same time to perform an essentially decorative function.

The idea here is not to define a perfect, finished space with a place for everything and everything in its place, but to furnish an ambience where the rooms enjoy a degree of freedom, with layouts which are the result of daily routines rather than of planning with military precision.

In this way, the old and the new come together in an almost random fashion, obeying neither hierarchies nor rules. A crumbling wall or worn beam become as important to the house as a specially-designed piece of furniture.

The first concern of rehabilitation is to respect the given circumstances. A space does not need to be rebuilt to bring it up to date (in many cases this would be its death knell); it needs to be looked at with new eyes and reassessed.

The piano is a romantic element to temper the rather cold ambience of the study.

The study is a reinterpretation of the traditional office.

Open spaces

This is an interior of open plan but interrelated spaces, in which the original, avant-garde structure of the building seems to assume the leading role. The furniture is minimal, but sufficient — the only pieces that have been used are those whose absence would make living in the house uncomfortable — and the rooms created astonish by virtue of their serenity and studied minimalism.

In the living room, the major feature is a spectacular exposed-brick vaulted ceiling. In order not to eclipse the beauty of this architectural resource, simple furniture has been selected in discreetly neutral tones. Only an easy chair and a foot-stool, both upholstered in a rich, bright red, break the colour monotony.

The structural divisions between areas appear to be flexible, almost provisional. Wooden partitions separate the living area from the rooms on either side, with wide sliding doors to provide access between one and the other.

The kitchen is in pale wood and brushed stainless steel, with a slate floor. The study holds only a desk, chair and wall-hung bookshelves; the bedroom is as simple as a monastic cell.

Decorating a home with a large floor area using only a few basic elements and leaving many open spaces is a risky option. In this case the gamble has paid off, and the overall ambience of the house is one of simple and aesthetic comfort.

Wooden partitions, with an integral sliding door, separate the different rooms.

The furniture in the living room has been carefully selected to enhance the simple beauty of the architectural structure.

Secluded corners

Not so long ago the bathroom was considered to be a private area, usually discreetly concealed. Today it often tends to be exhibited; money is lavished on it and it is sometimes taken as an indicator not only of the owners' taste, but also financial status.

In the interior on the facing page, the bathroom has ceased to be taboo to the extent that it forms an active part of the bedroom itself. A partial partition, open on one side, provides some privacy to the area containing the bath and the basin. The w.c. is concealed behind the bright blue door at the rear.

The second bathroom on these pages is designed to take into account the sloping ceiling of an attic. On the wall behind the basin is a made-to-measure cupboard, with numerous drawers and containers that offer a considerable amount of storage in a very compact space.

The sanitary ware and bath are in white, as is the vanity unit top, which adds a crisp, clean feeling to the room. To ensure that it does not appear too cold and aseptic, a natural polished wood floor and the amber-coloured cupboard fronts and counter detailing add some necessary colour and warmth.

The bathrooms presented here are both simple and uncluttered, but are also very personal and welcoming. Their elements are carefully planned within the available space, and both areas have been designed to offer a feeling of quiet elegance.

The cupboard and the wall cladding have been fitted around the slope of the ceiling.

This bathroom forms part of the main bedroom itself, with just a partial screen for privacy.

Warm wood

Wood is used everywhere in this house, giving the interior a unity and a warm glow that only this, the most natural of materials, is able to provide.

The staircase, one of the main elements of the interior structure, acts both as a means of circulation and to divide the space. On the ground floor, it separates a small living room from an open area used as an improvized art gallery. The living area is furnished with a starkly white sofa with two matching armchairs and a stylized side table. On the natural stone floor, a set of brightly patterned Oriental rugs adds some colour and softness. In the exhibition space, a cool, sky-blue wall provides a beautiful contrast to the rich warmth of the polished wood.

At the top of the stairs, the wood doors are discreetly integrated into the structure to the point where they seem to become almost invisible.

The staircase is not only a means of circulation, but is also used to separate the different areas.

The stark simplicity of the living room is softened by the brightly patterned Oriental rugs.

But perhaps the most unusual area in this home is the bathroom, with its very modern, innovative design. Again, wood is used to cover walls and ceiling, interrupted only by the ceramics of the sanitary ware and the glass mirror. A central column breaks the space, creating different visual planes. In case an excess of wood should make the room appear too dark and gloomy, in the ceiling there is a huge sky-light that floods the entire bathroom with natural light.

To use so much wood within every room of this house could have been rather oppressive and resulted in loss of clarity in some of the interiors. To prevent this from happening, the designer has offset its dominant visual presence by adding areas of bright, clear colour, installing a selection of eye-catching modern furniture, and making clever use of natural light.

At the top of the stairs, the doors are entirely integrated into the wooden structure.

An excess of wood could have made the bathroom appear small, but the large mirror and the flood of natural light from the skylight counteract this feeling.

Attention
to detail

It is attention to detail that makes the difference between good and bad design. However, sometimes this detailing goes unnoticed — even though it may be important to the smooth running of the home — just because it does not fall in one of the main rooms of the house.

These photographs show storage systems within a corridor and the rather unusual entrance to a bathroom. It is unlikely that one would consider any of these to be the most remarkable feature of the particular home that they appear in, yet they are still vitally important because they are situated in very small spaces into which a variety of other fixtures, furnishings, and electrical appliances also have to be fitted.

The wooden storage system appears to float in the space, as it is surrounded by glass. The transparent strips above and below it allow us to see the space in its entirety, while at the same time ensuring a visual separation between the passage and the rooms on the far side.

The entrance to the bathroom is a tremendously subtle detail; it is covered with glazed mosaic as though it were part of the wall. One could almost walk past it without noticing that it was there. However, the marble flooring used in the bathroom is then taken under the door and right across the corridor, indicating the presence of the bathroom in a less obvious fashion, while at the same time breaking up the length of the corridor.

Glazed blue mosaic tiles are not only used to clad the outside of the bathroom, but are also used on the walls and shower cubicle inside.

A temple of peace

The floor at this end of the room is in blue ceramic tiling, picking up the bright colour of the scattered wall tiles.

The bathroom shown in these pages has been designed as a temple devoted to the care of the body. Its generous dimensions provide plenty of room for manoeuvre and its plain and simple style encourages relaxation.

The walls and much of the floor area are clad in small, neutral stone-coloured tiles, interspersed with the odd sky-blue tile to add a discreet touch of colour and detail. The built-in units are very modern, without being remotely avant-garde. The pale wood of the fittings, the same material as used for the bathroom door, endows the room with a certain youthful freshness. The polished marble top features two wash-basins, while a mirror occupies the entire wall above, visually duplicating the space.

At the opposite end of the bathroom, the bath has been made into an unusual feature that endows the whole room with a certain distinction and character: a large, round bath set on a raised platform under a big window. The bathing area is flooded with natural light, while the occupant of the bath can enjoy the views through the window. The raised platform is clad in the same tiles as the walls and floor, as are the two wide steps leading up to the bath. On one side of the platform, a glazed partition is fitted to separate this area from the shower area.

So with just a few basic elements, and with the same tiles throughout the space as a unifying factor, this bathroom design is very simple, but the overall effect is both grand and inviting.

The bathing area is the star attraction in this room.

Urban landscapes

The three rooms featured on these pages are very different; they share neither style, colours, nor design solutions. Even so, there is one factor that unites them: all three have an 'urban' feel, since they abound in straight lines, metallic elements and neutral tones.

First the bathroom, which features very straight lines instead of the rounded forms normally found in this kind of room. The room seems to be double its actual size because of the large wall mirror with recessed lights above.

Next comes an angular-looking kitchen, with a long, narrow strip of window making the most of the cityscape beyond. Artificial light is provided by a number of recessed lights strategically placed in the ceiling. The kitchen appliances and cabinets are under a white worktop that unifies the area.

The main picture shows part of a former warehouse that has been refurbished as a home. In this room, which acts as a kitchen-dining room, the curve of the vaulted ceiling is highlighted with concealed spotlights, and provides a feeling of space. The store cupboards are part wooden, part metallic, light and adaptable, while the dining-room table consists of a sheet of glass resting on a steel frame.

To make the most of an urban interior, it should recreate, as these do, aspects of city reality. The resulting image is at once modern and very masculine.

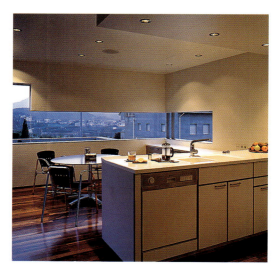

Straight lines replace the traditional rounded forms in this bathroom.

This kitchen is also characterized by straight lines and the total absence of purely decorative elements.

Wood, metal and glass: three highly modern materials used to decorate an old warehouse.

Dazzling white

White reflects light; it is the colour of innocence, hope and joy. It elevates the senses and creates an ambience of calm elegance untouched by the passage of time, since it is rarely affected by the whimsical dictates of fickle fashion.

In these two rooms, white is used as the basic theme. Although the decorative resources employed in each are different, both glow with light reflected by the white walls and furniture.

In the sitting room on the facing page, the pale gleam of the parquet floor softens the visual impact of the white. The room is somewhat irregular in shape, defined by the dwelling's façade which features a number of impressive arched windows. A sofa for three, a chaise longue and an armchair occupy most of the space. Instead of a traditional bookshelf, there is a light, wall-hung unit.

In the room below, white predominates: only the rugs and the iron fireplace break the overall uniformity. The false ceiling that conceals a number of spotlights is one of the room's main features: it seems to be a continuation of the window blinds on each side and provides clear, transparent light. The decor is completed with two large sofas and two or three modern chairs.

Both these rooms have a peaceful and relaxing atmosphere, much of which comes from the absence of colour, but they are neither bland nor boring.

Here the white is less stark, being softened by the parquet floor and the shades of off-white in the upholstery.

Highly personal

In order for a bedroom to reflect the personality of its owners, only a few details are needed. The colour of the walls, the texture of the fabrics, the design of the furniture — each tiny element has its part to play, defining a personal style and establishing specific decorative criteria.

Discreet and relaxing, this bedroom uses different pastel shades of blue, combined with brilliant white. The mixture is so cleverly done that all the colours seem to merge into one another, creating wonderful nuances.

All that can be seen of the bed itself is the headboard — two large squares of wood — and one of its metal legs. It is covered with practical, elegant linen, sober and urbane. The bedspread in particular is the most vivid note of colour in the room, breaking up what could be seen as aesthetic monotony. The tables on either side of the bed match the headboard, while the elegant white easy chair with its wooden trim ties in with the rest of the decor. The picture leaning against the wall adds another, rather quirky, personal note, as does the small piece of sculpture on one bedside table and the model dog on the other.

This interior's main virtue is the careful arrangement of furniture and ornament, which together create an incomparable balance. The different elements adapt to the garret-like space, creating a serene ambience that faithfully reflects the owner's character.

Without the bright blue of the bedspread adding richness and brightness, this room would be almost stark.

The unusual wooden headboard is one of the main features of the room.

Living spaces

The spaces inside this dwelling are neither fixed nor rigid; on the contrary, the interior creates an impression of movement and change, of restless dynamism.

Areas interrupt each other, creating new spaces that, while perfectly well-defined, are at once linked and separated. In the study-library, for example, different visual planes are superimposed on one another. The tall, wall-to-wall storage unit and shelving meets a vaulted bridge across the back of the area, which creates a new flow of movement. On the bridge, high up in the background, we glimpse a new room with its own bookshelf.

The bedroom is severely minimalist in design, being almost completely bare and empty. Wood is used to cover both floors and walls, with the single exception of one wall in exposed brick. On the floor, the bed is a comfortable futon on a tatami.

Another room is vaguely Oriental in style, with an abundance of rugs, twisted paper lampshades and a wicker chair, whose sinuous form recalls the silhouette of a striking cobra.

Given the strong architectural character of this house the decor must take second place, being required merely to elegantly offset the structure, neither concealing nor masking it.

The bedroom is severely minimalist in style.

Ethnic crafts and rich accent colours give this corner a distinctly exotic feeling.

The bookshelf meets a vaulted bridge that creates a new space.

The mediterranean spirit

This bright and fresh bedroom has a distinctly Mediterranean feel. The clean, simple colours — white walls and floor, the pale sand-coloured wood of the furniture and the bright blue details — are the colours of a Mediterranean beach.

The bed is simple in design, with a plain base in the same pale-coloured wood as the side unit, but it looks soft and inviting. Instead of bedside tables there are two rectangular niches cut into the walls, one on each side of the bed, containing shelves. Overall the room is very modern, but it has some period touches — for instance the colonial-style fan that hangs from the ceiling. On the wall, an abstract painting provides a touch of bright colour.

The wall-to-wall, sliding glass doors flood the room with light, but the quality and intensity of the light can be tempered by adjusting the two roller blinds. These are also white, but have been coated to protect them against salt spray. In case these blinds might seem too prosaic and functional, spoiling an otherwise beautiful,

almost ethereal ambience, there are also soft, filmy, romantic curtains.

The white marble of the floor becomes white-painted decking over the threshold, on the terrace outside. The transition is so gentle, however, that interior and exterior seem to be almost one.

The quality of the light in coastal areas can be so intense that light becomes the main protagonist, flooding the room and creating its own ambience.

The wall-to-wall sliding glass doors means that the room is flooded with natural light.

The abstract painting on the wall adds a touch of brilliant colour.

A summer house

The simple dining room has a distinctly urban feel.

With its ceramic flooring, cool upholstery and absence of any carpet, this living-dining room seems to have been designed for use during hot summer days. It is a room of clean, relaxing beauty, characterized by a certain economy of elements and discreet neutral colours.

Large glass doors occupy two of the walls, through which natural light pours, bouncing off the white surfaces that abound in the room. The living area is the very essence of simplicity, the furniture consisting of a large sofa, three easy chairs and a foot-stool, all in white. In the middle, a clear glass table stands on sturdy legs. Behind the sofa there is a bookcase in wood and glass.

The dining area, like the living room, shuns decorative excess and vivid colours. The sober rectangular table is surrounded by simple chairs with plain blue upholstery, an aesthetic typical of modern offices. At the far end, against the wall, a sideboard presides over the room.

This is a supremely harmonious room, designed in soft, neutral tones combined with clever touches of bright colour here and there that prevent it from becoming too bland.

Although the area is not a large one, both the dining and living areas seem very spacious and comfortable, an effect that has been produced by cutting back the quantity of furniture to the minimum.

Since the glass coffee table is transparent it seems to visually disappear, making the seating area appear more spacious.

Top of the hill

The bright orange wall adds depth to the room.

This house enjoys an enviable site on top of a hill, with the city at its feet. Decorative elements have been reduced to a minimum, to allow full attention to be given to the high-quality architectural structure.

Shown on the facing page is the living room. This opens onto a terrace, the edge of which is defined only by a low kerb so as not to restrict the magnificent view of the city. Both the living room ceiling and the large door to the terrace consist of a framework of wooden slats and glazed surfaces, creating an interplay of light and shadow to captivate the sensitive observer. A yellow three-seat sofa, a bench in the same colour and a wooden centre table are the only pieces of furniture. Other elements were superfluous and might have concealed the beauty of the exceptional architectural environment.

In the bedroom, the colours used create different visual planes that are surprising and pleasing. Three walls are bright, clean white, the fourth wall has been painted in an unusual bitter orange. Besides breaking the chromatic unity, the orange wall acts as the centre of interest and adds depth to the room. The wardrobes have been installed on either side of the entrance, like columns marking a portal.

Simple, uncluttered environments with the minimum of furniture leave a large amount of free space, which both looks elegant and enhances the constructional quality of the dwelling.

The living room opens onto a large terrace, which has only a low kerb to make the most of the view.

A rustic flavour

A series of unusual, eye-catching details arranged against either an ochre or a red background turn this house into a constant succession of surprises. The eye-catching bed, with its canopy hanging down on either side; the small round tables in the living room, which could almost have been taken from a magic show; and particularly the fireplace, clad with blue mosaic and partly painted with vertical blue and orange stripes — a detail that is picked up from the sofa upholstery.

The bathroom is worthy of particular attention. Rather larger in size than these spaces tend to be, with the privilege of having a window to let in daylight, this room ceases to be a utilitarian space for a hurried wash before rushing off to work and becomes an inviting area in which to relax and enjoy life.

The surface surrounding the wash basins and the low wall around the bath tub are of brick clad with a reddish stucco similar in tone to that used in the bedroom. A large wall-to-wall mirror runs above the wash basins to visually duplicate the space. The mirror is bordered by a strip of blue mosaic; the same material is also used to clad the bath. The open shelving on the wall makes a display feature of all the paraphernalia that needs to be on hand in a bathroom.

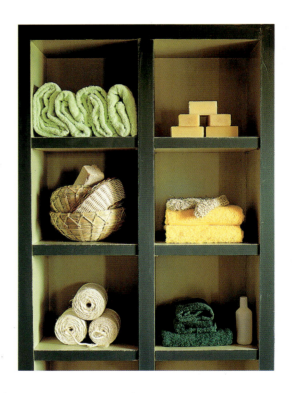

Detail of the open shelving on the bathroom wall.

The living room and the bathroom.

The master bedroom, with its eye-catching bed.

Power to the imagination

The daring design of this unusual room introduces vivid colours with restraint and creates spaces at once useful and tremendously original.

The room itself is arranged as a living room and library. The main elements are placed on the periphery leaving the centre free and empty, thus clearing what could otherwise appear to be a very cramped space. An overall glance at the room reveals that what is most outstanding is the masterful use of colour, combining rather subdued tones with vivid ones, disguising defects and accentuating virtues. Thus, for example, the marble flooring that has seen better days seems to be revived by the colourful vitality of the sofas and the bright Oriental rugs.

At one end of the room a metal spiral staircase leads down to the floors below. The staircase continues up into this room, creating a kind of viewing platform. The area to one side forms the library, and holds a large wooden bookcase carefully fitted into the confines of the space. The walls have been painted a pale yellow, tempered here and there by panels of rich burnt orange.

The use of daring colours and original structures is what makes this interior so special and unconventional. This kind of personal and innovative decor makes the most of what could have been a rather boring and insipid space.

The bright upholstery of the sofa is one of the main splashes of colour in the room.

The small library makes the most of the odd space next to the staircase.

Reflections in glass

The platform which forms the base of the bed is extended along the wall to form a large desk at the opposite end.

The main interiors in this home, specifically a dining room and youthful bedroom, are spaces of subdued elegance and feature interesting decorative solutions.

The corridor is integrated into the dining area, and on the side wall a row of vertical modules has been placed, like a row of columns, each joined to the next by three shelves to form an elegant storage unit. The wood that covers walls, ceiling and floor unifies the environment and provides a natural warmth. One of the dining room walls has been replaced by a translucent glass partition that glows with light and is full of beautiful reflections. The table is a plain and simple rectangle, accompanied by four matching, upholstered chairs.

The bedroom features a most original design solution to the problem of needing both sleeping and study space in a small area. The bed platform is extended along the wall to become a large, comfortable desk at its far end. This is possible because the room is structured across two different levels. Wood is also used in the bedroom, although not to the same extent as in the dining room.

Originality is not something exclusive to avant-garde interiors. As this home shows, it is possible to be very innovative without being too audacious.

The corridor is integrated into the dining room, and both areas are completely clad in wood.

Making full use of the space

These days it is quite difficult to find a large home with spacious rooms. In many cases people have to be content with apartments of rather modest dimensions, in which they must fit furniture and all kinds of personal objects without causing absolute disorder.

The first thing that strikes the visitor to this pleasant home is the fact that the spaces are open and one has room to breathe, despite the fact that every spare inch has been exploited. The secret of its success lies in the removal of rigid barriers and the creation of interrelated rooms that share spaces and colours. The corridor not only acts as a central walkway, leading to a totally open-plan kitchen, but is also used as a practical storage area.

The rooms are delineated with partial partitions, which also act as storage units. For instance, in one of the bedrooms the partition becomes a bookcase on its inner side. The high ceiling in this particular room has also made it possible to build a small mezzanine floor.

Colour and different materials perform an important function in this interior: that of differentiating between environments. White walls stand opposite yellow ones, divided by ultramarine partitions. Parquet gives way to dark ceramic flooring in the kitchen area.

It takes great talent and attention to detail to take full advantage of minimum spaces. In this case, all the interiors have been designed and planned with great skill, creating extra square footage where there seemed to be none.

The kitchen is totally open-plan, with no space wasted.

A long bookshelf has been built in the corridor that leads into the different rooms.

Overlooking the sea

Beside the everchanging sea stands this refreshing, youthful home, characterized by an abundance of well-exploited corners and the exemplary use of decorative resources.

The interior echoes the placid beauty of the house exterior; the rooms impress the visitor with their atmosphere of welcoming hospitality and tremendously vitality. As in much modern architecture, the different spaces are united and interrelated.

The main task of the interior designer is usually to interpret the spirit and character of a home's future occupants. In the case of a holiday home, an apartment on the coast or a mountain hide-away, the owners may specifically want the decor to suggest a different mood and alternative habits. In such cases, the decorator should not be concerned so much with the owners' everyday habits as with their aspirations when they escape from the routine of work and city for a few days. This philosophy extends to certain rooms being suited to a specific time of year or even particular weather conditions.

There are rooms which have no meaning without an overcast, rainy sky pressing against the curtains; living rooms which look incomplete without sunlight bouncing

Large windows offer exceptional views of the wonderful coastal landscape.

This bedroom is concealed behind a moveable partition.

off the walls and kitchens that lose heart when the spring thaw starts and their fire goes out.

A holiday home for use in the summer months is precisely what the designer has achieved here. The apartment's freshness and simplicity give it a youthful feel, while its clear, fluid, colour-packed spaces actively encourage a less conventional, more relaxed attitude to life, particularly suited to occupation in the summertime, when everything takes on a lighter, more relative meaning.

Partial wooden partitions, stained bright red, meet walls whose brickwork is lightly disguised beneath a thin coat of whitewash. A spacious and ultra-modern living room has just a few well-designed pieces of furniture in simple, neutral colours, creating a simple, unobtrusive background against which one can relax. This area gives way to a cheerful dining room, in which pieces of brightly-coloured furniture are set against others entirely in white. All the surfaces are easy to clean and maintain, to conserve the time and energy required for such every-day mundane tasks.

Each of the rooms is unpretentious and harmonious, allowing the fabulous views of the sea that can be seen through the windows full prominence in the ongoing life of the house.

The dining room is bright and cheerful, with its rich colours and simple shapes.

The wall behind the sofa is decorated with asymmetrically arranged pictures.

The industrial-style kitchen, dominated almost completely by stainless steel, is carefully planned into the rather cramped dimensions of a narrow passageway. Despite its small area, it contains all that could be needed to cook and store food.

The bathroom is entirely clad in wood, except for the shower which has tiled walls and is hidden behind a glass partition. The rich colours used in this room give it a feeling of intimacy and warmth.

Since holiday homes are only used for part of the time, the designer can afford to be more dramatic and use strong colours and unusual effects that might pall in everyday use. This home is particularly notable for its vibrant colour schemes and strong design statements.

The industrial-style kitchen may be compact, but it holds all one may need to cook and store food.

The bathroom is simple and stylish, with bright colours and easy-to-clean surfaces.

A trio of aces

These three uncommonly elegant interiors exhibit rhythm, harmony and balance. They are not only original in design, but also overcome their spatial limitations with imagination and good taste.

On the facing page is a dining room, characterized by its atmosphere of being an avant-garde conference hall: an empty space of very generous dimensions with dramatic architectural details. The parquet floor offsets the deliberate coldness of the room, a coldness increased by the large stretch of glass blocks set in one of the walls, through which the light penetrates, tempered by mysterious transparencies. The table chosen is a rectangular model with a granite top, while the accompanying chairs are light, simple and black. Against the glass-block wall two paintings, an old trunk and two Charles Rennie Mackintosh chairs are set, as if in transit to some other location in the building.

Below left is a space that is part of a larger room: a small sitting area has been created between two doors that open onto the exterior. Although this is basically a zone of passage, it has been endowed with great intimacy. The stove with its open flue running up the wall and the two reed upholstered easy chairs on either side create an area that is very inviting.

Finally, this bedroom leads seamlessly off a corridor, the parquet flooring and walls painted the same colour as those of the corridor creating a smooth transition. The bed is a simple model with a round headboard, beside which stands a stylized metal bedside table.

The attractiveness of these serene, well-balanced spaces lies above all in their simplicity and visual cleanliness.

A zone of passage has been transformed into an intimate sitting area.

The corridor almost seems to be an extension of the bedroom.

The dramatic architectural features of this room are emphasized by simplicity of decoration.

An interior full of life

Cheerful, youthful colours, gentle contrasts and sharply designed furniture work together here to create a bright interior that exudes vitality and freshness.

The different areas of this living-dining room are separated by an arrangement of panels and false partitions that define the areas without closing them off. As a whole, the room is a space of great beauty in which the furniture and accessories are arranged in a logical, balanced way.

The full zone devoted to living and dining is delineated on one side by a large, pale wood storage wall, on another by a blue partition — which conceals a practical kitchen — and on a third by the terrace doors. A rectangular table on metal legs emerges from the storage wall, set round with six simple white chairs. The clean, straight lines of storage and table are in contrast to the flamboyant curves of the enormous pumpkin-like ceiling light made of thin sheets of wood.

In the living area, the furniture consists of two springy, white sofas with a wood and glass table set between them. Natural light is tempered by roller blinds on the glass doors opening onto the exterior.

Outstanding among the many merits of this interior is the way in which the kitchen is hidden away from view, enclosed inside blue panels that also become an active part of the decor.

Overall view of the living-dining room, showing how the two areas relate.

A rectangular table with steel legs emerges from the storage wall.

Living in a warehouse

Beneath a curving vaulted roof lit with concealed spotlights lies a huge living room. As a former warehouse this was once a rather cold and unwelcoming space, but the designer has transformed it into a genuine home.

The large main room is divided into two different environments: a living room and dining room/kitchen. At the far end, lined with a number of panels and cupboards, a long corridor leads towards the garden. The living area is furnished with two large blue sofas on tiny castors. Between them, like a mobile sculpture, is a chest, also on castors, full of unusual silver spheres. Opposite, an old wooden box acts as the television trolley.

The kitchen design falls somewhere between industrial and futurist. Stainless steel predominates, and its structures are light and functional. Everything is arranged in rows, leaving room for a central table. The style of the dining room matches that of the kitchen.

Warehouses refurbished as homes are difficult to decorate; due to their massive floor area they can seem impersonal. Here, thanks to carefully-chosen furniture and the correct spatial distribution, a warm and very welcoming interior has been created.

Overall view of the living area, with the kitchen and dining area in the background.

A corridor lined with storage leads away to the garden.

White on white

A large room decorated entirely in white is very dramatic and makes a fabulous background for bold shapes and simple styling.

Against white walls and on floors of the same colour white furnishings are set. The only touch of colour is provided by the rich, bright designs of the Oriental rugs. A row of classical busts depicting emperors of old, which are set on carved marble columns, creates an atmosphere that is reminiscent of Roman forums and luxurious patrician residences.

The room is rectangular in plan, with huge windows opening into a garden on either side. The light is controlled by adjusting horizontal blinds, the strong lines of which are echoed in the ceiling slats. Standing against one wall is an iron fireplace, around which a generous modern sofa, a chesterfield-type sofa and a small occasional table are gracefully arranged. At one end, the dining room contains only

This area, with its small classical sofa, leads to other rooms in the house.

The horizontal blinds on the large side windows are linked visually to the false ceiling.

a small, light, round table accompanied by three metal chairs with upholstery covers.

Near the fireplace, there is a small area concealed behind white garden railings and a heavy curtain. The curtain is draped to one side and held back by a garland of leaves. Behind the railings stands a small classical sofa, again entirely in white.

The restrained classicism of this room takes the visitor back to previous periods dominated by cold elegance and the absence of colour. Nevertheless, this style has been interpreted according to present day taste: it has been carefully updated and all hint of incoherence or anachronism very skilfully avoided.

The curtain is held back with a garland of leaves, in keeping with the garden-room design.

The white room contains both living area and dining area. The Oriental rugs create the sole splash of vivid colour, echoed here in the fruit and flowers on the table.

Sobriety
and colour

The bathroom is discreetly decorated. The light-coloured parquet floor unites the two adjoining rooms.

Bare brick walls are the main feature in this austere, sober bedroom, which contains only a few basic elements. Bright colour, introduced in small doses, adds to the dramatic visual effect without being overwhelming.

The sturdy wall against which the bed is placed reaches up to a false ceiling with discreet lighting. The furniture is reduced to just the indispensable elements: the wooden bed with rectangular headboard and a plain and simple bedside table, both of excellent quality. The accessories thus acquire vital importance, for without them the bedroom would perhaps appear too simple. The fuchsia-coloured bedspread, the set of patterned pillows and the boxes on the table provide a note of bright, youthful colour, offsetting the severity of the rest of the room. Warm wood flooring links the bedroom to an elegant bathroom, which is decorated with light tones and polished surfaces.

The predominant cream colour used in the bathroom is very suitable for a rather dark space. The room contains a single washbasin, while the shower is concealed behind a glass partition.

Careful lighting makes the most of the touches of colour in both rooms, as well as enhancing the beauty of the contrasting textures in the rough brick and smooth, polished wood.

The pillows and the fuchsia-coloured bedspread are important details to liven up this otherwise rather severe bedroom.

Adapting to the environment

The main aim of design should be, above all, to adapt to and improve upon real conditions. Therefore the designer must study the available space, analyze the possibilities of different rooms and draw up designs capable of making the most of each individual case.

Shown below is a modern kitchen, arranged beneath the curved vaulted roof of a former warehouse. The design uses wood, steel and glass, with many straight lines to contrast with the curved surface of the ceiling. The main kitchen appliances are hidden away in a cupboard embedded into the wall. The centre of the room is occupied by a long table with steel legs.

A rather surprising note in this very modern environment is the introduction of a number of rustic details, such as the wicker baskets and the bouquets of dried flowers. The dark linoleum flooring in the kitchen changes to parquet in the dining area next door.

On the facing page is the utility room in the same warehouse home. Again, the overall feel is very modern, counteracted with rustic wicker baskets and bunches of dried herbs. This is a small space but the designer has made the most of it, using the height of the area with tall cupboards and suspended storage. The ironing table is set across the area, utilizing the light from the glazed door.

The industrial-style kitchen lies beneath the vaulted roof of a former warehouse.

A number of rustic elements have been introduced into an essentially modern environment.

The search for balance

The available space in this house has been logically and sensibly exploited to create an orderly, comfortable and very functional living space. Balance characterizes each corner of the house, providing a dynamism that, though desirable, is not always that easy to achieve.

The first floor is a huge room divided into different areas: a comfortable living room, a dining room and a study or work area. One wall of the living-room is taken up with a wide wooden bookcase, in the centre of which there is a movable panel on rails. The seating arrangement consists of two large white sofas and a rocking chair in the same colour.

The remaining areas in the room are arranged around the open metal staircase. The study with its striking translucent table

The wide bookcase, with its sliding central panel, is a major feature of the living room.

The translucent glass table in the study is both unusual and striking.

is on one side, on the other is the dining room for eight, with a rectangular glass table and a set of wooden chairs. Next to the study there is also another small dining table for four, with upholstered chairs.

Colours are all soft and neutral, and the overall ambience of the room is modern and light. This same theme is carried through to the rest of the house, with extensive use of glass and steel.

A practical wardrobe with acid-etched glass doors.

The stair is the main element, around which different areas are arranged.

Open to the exterior

The blue cupboard draws the eye to the view outside.

This charming living room can be totally opened to the exterior by sliding back a large glazed door that gives onto the garden. The natural light that floods in from outside enhances the colours and textures in the room.

As a whole, the living room featured on these pages is balanced, serene and makes careful use of every square inch of space, overlooking no corners and avoiding dead spots. One of the walls is clad in wood, providing warmth and offsetting the white that predominates in the colour scheme. The only splash of true colour is the large, electric-blue cupboard situated next to the glass door.

The furniture in this room fundamentally consists of three visually striking pieces: two identical, large, blue and white striped sofas opposite each other, and a wooden

centre table with a glass top. A small touch of colour is provided by the ultramarine cushions placed on the sofas.

At the opposite end of the room, an acid-etched sliding glass door leads into a long corridor discreetly lit via recessed lights in the ceiling. The main element here is another large blue cupboard against one of the walls, which is totally adapted to the architectural characteristics of the corridor.

The main items of furniture are two sofas placed opposite each other, with a central table.

A maritime character

A study area has been created in the bedroom.

In a luminous setting, a blue and white transparent decor indicates the proximity of the sea and creates a refreshing maritime-style interior.

The living room featured on the facing page is flooded with translucent natural light and has a Mediterranean feel. The freshness it exudes is possibly due to the predominance of blue and white. The only other colours in the room come from the natural tones of the ceramic flooring, brick fireplace and wooden tables. The fireplace itself stands against one of the walls, its flue hidden in a plain chimney breast with no mantelpiece or surround. The fresh colours of a blue and white striped sofa, accompanied by a second sofa and an easy chair in plain blue, are echoed in the glass accessories on the central table and the occasional tables on either side.

The bedroom is painted the same colours as the living room. One corner has been given over to a small study or work area, with an old desk, a wall-to-wall bookcase and a comfortable sofa. At the other end of the room stands the huge double bed with a built-in headboard.

The strong light reflected off the sea has become one of the main elements in this design. It surely would not work as well in an urban setting, or where natural light was more limited.

The freshness of the living room is based on the use of two colours: blue and white.

Simple elegance

Space and light are the basic elements used in the design of this home, to create a simple, but very luxurious environment. The warm glow of the wood that covers the floor, and is also used for pieces of built-in furniture, contrasts with the cold, pure white of the ceiling, columns and walls.

At the far end of this room, a traditional iron stove is fitted with a polished steel flue, which reaches up through the double height space in the centre of the area. The polished surface of the flue is echoed in the metal rails around the opening on the floor above.

Structural columns always seem to fall in the wrong place, but here the designer has used one of them as the basis for a special storage unit, which holds books as it curves round the column and then drops to form a platform to hold the television. Ranged in front of this, both the central table and the chest acting as an occasional table are on wheels, allowing the layout to be amended at will.

At the far end of the room, the dining area holds a stylized rectangular table with a glass top and a set of garden-style chairs. The use of garden-style furniture further emphasizes the interplay between interior and exterior.

The bathroom is entirely clad in rich, bright blue mosaic tiles. Set against this, the plain, natural wood accessories in this room take on a new meaning, becoming elegant rather than austere.

The rich contrast between the warm wood floor and the cool blue upholstery is one of the main elements in this design.

The bathroom is clad throughout with bright blue mosaic tiles.

Family life

Exceptionally warm, welcoming and homely, the interiors of this house seem to have been designed for family life. It is full of carefully-planned corners put to logical and practical use.

At the top of the stairs is first a small study with a built-in desk, wood-faced on the outside and of stainless steel inside.

Decorative objects are of great importance here, particularly the two candlesticks and the huge chess pieces. The parquet floor is the same colour as the desk, and the two low steps mark a further change in level.

In the bedroom what catches the eye is the large closet divided into two sections: one which contains hanging and the other with numerous drawers and shelves to take folded clothes.

It is easy to overlook how much space is actually needed to store everything away. Yet, by planning ahead to achieve plenty of storage space for everything required and rationalizing clothing and possessions, it is easy to keep everything ship-shape. Not just the bedroom, but all the other rooms in the house could benefit from the existence of spaces which are exclusively designed to store things away.

Old houses often contain rooms without a specific function, and these are often the ones which end up being most used. They become wardrobes, junk rooms, workshops or darkrooms: modern houses could take a leaf out of their book.

A small study stands at the top of the stair.

The massive closet planned side-on to the wall is the most outstanding element in this bedroom.

A cheerful awakening

The pictures make a feature of the traditional white tiling.

There is nothing better than to wake up in the morning and start the day with a good breakfast: it cheers the spirit and prepares one for the hardest day's work. Here are two interiors, a youthful bedroom and a refreshing kitchen with the table laid, both of which are capable of raising the spirits first thing in the morning.

Full advantage has been taken of the bedroom's tiny dimensions. It is decorated in warm ochre and yellow and the bed is covered with a romantic voile mosquito net, giving a very colonial feeling.

The end of the bed reaches the desk, so there is no need for a headboard. This desk occupies the entire length of one wall, and is placed before a wide window with translucent glass, doing away with the need for curtain or blind. Bookshelves hang from one of the walls.

The kitchen has been decorated with pictures hanging on the wall, on top of the traditional white tiling. The furniture, also white, is arranged in rows and the table is placed in the centre. Light penetrates the room through three windows, beneath which numerous storage jars are displayed on a shelf.

These interiors are examples of how to make the best use of limitations. The tiny spaces are packed with elements that have little or no relation to each other, but have a deeply emotional meaning to their owner. The overall effect, however, is not of disconnected jumble but of a very harmoniously arranged space.

This bedroom may be very tiny, but it holds all that one may need.

Around the fireplace

The different elements that provide this pleasant, spacious living room with its character have been arranged around an iron fireplace. In the middle, a large wooden cupboard partially conceals the kitchen.

The white walls, pale wooden furniture and the blue and white tapestries stand out against the black slate floor. The living space is delineated by a wooden bookcase against which a comfortable sofa stands, piled high with cushions. The seating arrangement is completed by two folding, upholstered chairs and two simple stools. A coffee table, made of two thick sheets of wood, stands in the centre of these pieces on a sisal rug. On the other side of the cupboard is the narrow galley kitchen. At one end, room has been found for a small table and four wicker chairs.

Three environments in a single space: living room, kitchen and dining room, all of them decorated in the same bright and cheerful style.

To the right is the large cupboard that separates the living room from the kitchen.

The iron fireplace is the focal point of the room.

Upstairs
downstairs

This house has only as many doors as are absolutely necessary. This does not mean that the rooms are any less independent; it is merely a result of the intelligent planning of the house's layout and structure over two floors.

Since the early decades of this century, fluidity of space has been one of the great paradigms of modern architecture and design. New technical possibilities saw the introduction of structures that were open, freer and less sub-divided than those using traditional building techniques. At the same time, as habits became more liberal, the demand for this type of space grew. Irrespective of either their advantages or their drawbacks, houses with large open-plan spaces and communicating rooms without doors continue to be a synonym of modernity, liberal habits and progressive ideas. This house also features another essential characteristic of the twentieth century: the supremacy of natural light and brightness. Well-lit, well-ventilated houses are just as important for psychological well-being as for physical health.

The house featured in these pages can be described as natural, healthy, light, and peaceful. This is a sure sign that the designer has succeeded in creating an interior with an atmosphere of well-being, naturalness and modernity. There are only a few details and items of furniture in this room, but each is unusual in itself — the metal fireplace set in front of the windows to the terrace, the glass side to the staircase, the semi-circular wicker sofa — and is chosen to create a coherent whole. The aim is a homogeneous image, rather than objects that need to be appreciated on an individual basis.

The same materials and finishes are picked up in different rooms throughout the house: light-coloured wood, white-painted walls, floors in different shades of ochre (honey-coloured sandstone on the ground floor and wood on the top floor), white upholstery and blinds, large glazed surfaces both outside and in. The overall effect is stunningly simple, yet at the same time has much to hold the eye.

Detail of the metal fireplace, which stands beside the great windows overlooking the terrace.

Two views of the kitchen. Once again, wood is the main material chosen and the room is almost stark in its simplicity.

Instead of handles, the doors to the fitted cupboard in the bedroom are equipped with small finger slots.

The staircase leads from the living room directly into the master bedroom.

Welcoming
ambiences

This home reflects the warm, vital, cheerful personality of its owners and is full of pleasant corners, either for private family life or for animated social gatherings. Everything is placed within reach, and the discreet ambience will adapt elegantly to the changes brought about by the passing of time.

Warm red, ochre and terracotta tones predominate in the living room: the rich colour of the polished wood parquet floor; the stuccoed walls; the large rug that lies diagonally on the floor. The two easy chairs are upholstered in ochre, while the sofas, lampshade and curtains introduce the complementary colour of heathery violet.

Throughout the house pictures, wall lamps or any other kind of decorative wall elements are very conspicuous by their absence. There are, in fact, pictures in the house, but all are propped up on shelves, side tables or chests of drawers rather than being hung on the wall. In this way, the walls stand out as clear, uncluttered areas, bold blocks of colour. In certain corners the occasional classic piece of furniture or artwork is placed, to offset the predominant modernity.

The false ceilings are used to conceal recessed lights in many areas, including the living room. Here the light from the standard lamp creates a pool of warm, golden light, while the cold light from the halogen directional spots in the ceiling is used to wash the walls and provide the background lighting.

This classic piece of furniture stands out against its very up-to-date surroundings.

Red, ochre and yellow tones predominate in the welcoming living room.

The cheerful, well-lit kitchen combines simple, pale wood units with metal handles and white lacquered furniture. The walls are mainly timber-clad, although those in the cooking area have been tiled in white for practicality. The room is big enough to hold a small round breakfast table, placed in the centre.

The plain bedroom, with access to a small ensuite bathroom, features a large double bed with a leather upholstered headboard and elegant white bedding.

Parquet flooring is laid all over the house, except in the kitchen and bathroom areas, to give a sense of continuity.

The bedroom is simple to the point of starkness.

A dining room leads off the kitchen, again in the same warm ochre colour scheme as the living room.

In a belvedere

The decor of this unusual home is entirely without barriers and open to the exterior. One of the walls is totally glazed, so that the entire space acts as a belvedere with stunning views of the fine surrounding landscape.

This house is very much influenced by its vertical rather than its horizontal layout. As the floors are limited in terms of space, it was decided to assign a single function to each of them.

The ground floor is the daytime area. A single large space provides the setting for all the family's joint activities in the course of the day: living room, dining room and kitchen area.

While this creates a feeling of openess, it also necessitates coherence in the choice of materials. Here, the leading role is taken by light-coloured wood, which is used for the floor, dining, coffee and occasional tables, shelves and kitchen cupboards, with only white and calming pale blue-grey as a counterpoint.

The living room area contains comfortable sofa and chairs arranged to make the most of the fantastic view, and a central table in the form of an elegant trolley. The dining area is also opposite the glazed wall and next to it is the kitchen, arranged in a 'U' shape. The kitchen itself is carefully planned to make the most of a rather limited space.

The dining room is located next to the glazed wall.

Living room, dining room and kitchen are contained in the same space.

The night-time area, with the bedrooms and bathrooms, occupies the entire upper floor of the house.

The functional-looking bedroom shown here has no aspirations to romanticism or theatricality and follows the same design theme of blue-grey and white, again with a pale wood parquet floor. The beauty of this simple, elegant room is based on economy of elements. The bed, with its soft upholstered headboard, is the main piece, although the unusual blue-painted cantilevered staircase that leads to a

mezzanine floor also catches the eye. A number of pictures are cleverly arranged on the floor, to leave the walls free as a plain colour statement.

The bathrooms again follow the same themes that have been set by the rest of the house. They are totally clad in vivid blue mosaic over both walls and floor, with white ceilings and sanitary ware, and pale wood storage units. They also feature acid-etched glass shower doors and translucent glass vanity shelves containing stainless steel washbasins.

The two main virtues of this home are its fully coordinated themes throughout the entire dwelling, and its complete openness to the exterior that makes the most of its stunning position.

A surprising element in the bedroom is the cantilevered staircase leading to a mezzanine floor over the bathroom.

The bathroom takes the theme set by the main spaces, but here the blue is emphasized.

Two original offices

Only too often, offices or studios in the home tend to be much too serious, conservative and even boring. But these days sobriety is not such a virtue, so freedom of expression, humour and originality have come to form part of this traditional kind of room.

The unusual character of an interior is sometimes a question of details. One of the offices shown here is a plain basic space, but it is filled with original elements: a desk equipped with castors so that it can be repositioned at whim in the room; an easy chair covered in printed fabric, slender shelves and an elegant stepped storage unit that also serves as a bookshelf.

Occasionally it is enough to choose an original piece of furniture, otherwise one could set the office in a space decorated in a somewhat incongruous way — for instance the impressive fresco that covers the walls of the classical studio. To highlight the unusual character of the fresco even more it has not been combined with furniture in a period style to match, but with classical modern items.

These two offices are very different in style, although they both enjoy the same good basic conditions — large dimensions, abundant light, a regular structure. In each case, full advantage has been taken of their individual qualities while shunning clichés and conventional concepts.

One of the most unusual elements here is the stepped storage unit used as a bookshelf.

The wall frescoes are the major feature of this interior.

Youthful freshness

Like a breath of fresh air, this small, welcoming living room seems to have been achieved almost as if by chance, effortlessly; something to which all successful decors should aspire. It is by no means that easy to achieve such natural-looking results, however. They invariably are the fruit of elaborate planning and design, since chance is not usually such a good counsellor.

All the elements in this living room seem to be balanced: spaces and volumes, colours and tones are masterfully combined to produce an environment in which the keynote is harmony. The walls, roller blinds and window frames are all white, which gives luminosity and a feeling of space. The upholstered furniture is also in tones of white, so that its outlines seem to merge with the overall atmosphere. The coffee table is in pale wood with a glass top. The bookcase, which holds books, records and personal memorabilia, and the side table are in the same wood. On the floor, a neutral sisal rug adds a note of freshness without attracting too much attention. Finally, the notes of colour, though few — the flowers, a couple of pictures — have been applied with precision. Thanks to them, this interior acquires life and character.

This fresh, youthful living room is basically neutral, with just a few touches of vivid colour.

The small bookcase is full of books, records and personal memorabilia.

Colour and fantasy

One of the study walls is entirely clad with paintings, drawings and photographs.

Nothing in this interior could be accused of being conventional. The changing colours across the walls, the separation of the spaces, the unusual architectural resources employed — the designer seems to have avoided the commonplace in search of new solutions, improvising with audacity and breaking away from anything already established.

In the centre of the large living-dining room is a curious structure: a staircase with asymmetrical brick steps, cutting across each other. As it rises, the brick gives way to a much lighter metal spiral staircase that disappears into the floor above.

In the living-dining room the walls are painted in varying shades of yellow. In the midst of so much colour, the furniture is discreet and does not attract too much attention. One of the walls features a large arch that frames a rectangular door and provides access to another room — a library or reading area. This is furnished with a desk and several folding canvas chairs. A most striking characteristic of this study is the fact that one of the walls is entirely covered with paintings, drawings and photographs of different sizes.

This interior has been decorated in an eclectic way, combining elements from a variety of provenances and in a wide range of colours. The result, nonetheless, is a tasteful combination that pleases the eye, and the walls also bear witness to the lives and hobbies of the house's owners.

The steps of the central stair also function as a small display area.

Everything is possible

Sometimes anything goes when designing an interior, and this one is a good example of the fact: from the deliberate peeling plaster on parts of the ceiling to the police cordon tape — used to seal off crime sites — which acts as a provocative garland. Nevertheless, the different elements, however surprising they may be individually, come together to create a balance, harmony and rhythm.

The space is very open, since there are hardly any barriers. The furniture, the cladding and the extraordinary murals that decorate the walls are used to indicate the limit of different areas. The structure of the interior improvises and plays with reality, offering partitions that overlap each other and gilt columns that provide a touch of dynamism. Garnet and yellow coloured diamonds have been painted on the bare concrete ceiling and the chaise longue sits against a low, gilded wall in the living area.

The library zone is more classic in its decor: the wooden bookshelf, the plain rectangular table, the rug and the leather easy chairs are those that would normally be found in traditional libraries. However, from the ceiling a metal grid is suspended with small shaded pendant lamps and, as a counterpoint to cliché and conventionality, a plastic cordon tape as used by the Barcelona City Police has been wound around the metal structure.

These details suggest that this living room has been designed almost as a huge three-dimensional collage rather than as an architectural space. The objects and ideas seem to have been taken from a variety of contexts, rather like a Dadaist composition, showing just how the designer has left his mark on this space.

A number of curious decorative elements counterbalance the classic style of the library.

In this open space, cladding, colours and murals are used to delineate the different areas.

An informal meeting

This elegant and very stylish living room is balanced and practical. Movement is easy between the different areas and everywhere a touch of informality has been maintained.

Generous dimensions and just a few pieces of furniture are the keys to this design. The basic plan is very simple: three very modern yellow leather armchairs arranged in the form of a cross and, in the middle, a low, light-coloured, wooden coffee table on a simple white rug.

One functional corner is structured as a self-contained leisure area for reading or listening to music, away from the main area. A Corbusier chaise longue is arranged in front of a special series of wall-hanging modules containing a hi-fi, with a standard lamp placed to throw a pool of light for reading.

Simple and discreet, the elements in this room have been arranged with skill and precision. The environment thus created is gently urbane and aesthetically attractive.

Some pieces of furniture, like the coffee table or the shelving modules that house the hi-fi, could have taken their inspiration from the sculptural work of American artist Donald Judd.

A corner away from the main area, for reading or listening to music.

This large and elegant room holds only a few pieces of classic furniture.

Daring elegance

Rich, warm colour is an integral part of this dwelling, enveloping it and giving rise to audacious contrasts. The warmth of the orange-stained wood that covers the floor — and is also used for pieces of built-in furniture and false partitions — contrasts with the cold, shining white of the ceiling and the delicacy of the pastel-blue wall. The living area has two large, comfortable, deep blue sofas and a matching easy chair, with a large glass coffee table in the centre. The dining area holds a rectangular glass table and a set of chairs with unusual wavy backs. Between each of the glass doors leading out into the garden, a set of curious modules that can be used as storage units have been placed.

One needs a large area to carry off the depth of colour used on the walls of this room. In a smaller area, it might make the space look even smaller. Even in this large living-dining room the fourth wall is pastel blue, to avoid any feeling of being in a box. The deep blue used on the sofas, being the complementary colour, makes the orange seem even richer.

Behind one of the sofas, a grand piano acts as an elegant, aesthetic counterpoint.

Strong contrasts create a vivid interior scheme.

On leaving this room, there is a circular wooden partition to one side that conceals another room. The panels that form this structure feature small windows placed in a vertical row, which offer a selection of tantalizing views of the very different space on the other side.

This interior is a fine example of colour used boldly and creatively, to achieve a scheme that is both elegant and daring at the same time.

The circular partition conceals another room. Through the open doors can be glimpsed a more conventional sitting room.

Unusual modules have been placed between the glass doors, to serve as storage units.

Similar
though different

These two washing areas are very similar in decorative style, but one is private while the other has been integrated into the bedroom.

Having a spacious dressing table and washing area right beside the bed is both practical and convenient. However, it can result in some difficult-to-solve design problems. Washing areas tend to be rather hard-edged and visually cold areas, while bedrooms need to be welcoming, relaxing and to reflect their owners' personality. In order to unite both environments, the designer must tone down the hardness of the washing area and design the bedroom so that it will tolerate a radically different area within itself. Thus, in one of these interiors the plain off-white walls of the bedroom become glazed soft-grey mosaic around the washing area, so it and the bedroom seem to meld into each other, giving rise to a new, functional and very unified room.

A series of highly personal touches gives the bedroom an informal air. There is the tall cylindrical box next to the bed that takes the place of a traditional bedside table, and the single lamp that hangs down on a lengthy flex from the ceiling – model Brera by Italian designer Achille Castiglioni – in place of the usual table or wall lamp by the bed.

The second bathroom on these pages is also clad in mosaic, although in this case the colour chosen is swimming-pool blue. This room features an interesting interplay of mirrors and both the bold water spout and the 'V' shaped vanity top that also acts as a water basin catch the eye. Bathrooms, like other spaces in the home, adapt to the needs and tastes of their users.

These two examples are based on the same decorative style, though each one has responded to different criteria: the first, to functionality and innovation; the second, to a wish to preserve privacy.

The 'V' shaped vanity top catches the water from the spout, so there is no need for a traditional wash basin.

This washing area is fully integrated into the bedroom.

A perfect layout

This kitchen shares the same space as a small dining room, although partial partitions and false walls clearly separate the two areas. By careful planning of individual elements, the designer has made the most of the generous spaciousness of this interior.

A long corridor totally clad in wood leads to the kitchen, although one might pass by it completely since its sliding doors are identical to the panels of the corridor. Once over the threshold, a very pleasant colour combination is revealed: glazed cream mosaic on the lower walls of the work area, with white walls above and a white ceiling, offset by the sudden contrast of the electric blue furniture and the garnet-red partition.

The elements in the kitchen zone are aligned against the walls, with cooking and washing-up areas standing opposite each other, thus allowing the user great freedom of movement. On the wall is a very modern set of metallic shelves, and the worktop itself is natural granite. The dining area is just on the other side of the garnet-red partition, and consists of an acid-etched glass-topped table with metal legs and four wooden chairs.

By integrating the kitchen and the dining room the former gains a feeling of elegance and the latter a degree of familiarity, even though the two areas are differentiated visually to highlight their different functions.

The garnet-red partition and the electric blue furniture stand out vividly against an otherwise harmonious whole.

The kitchen units are set around the wall, with the cooking and washing-up areas standing opposite each other.

A long, wood-panelled corridor leads to the kitchen.

Recovering the past

These rooms are in a spectacular art nouveau apartment, with very high ceilings and generous dimensions, which had unfortunately suffered from the harmful effects of the passage of time. However, with sensitive refurbishment, it has now recovered its past splendour, while adapting perfectly to today's needs and tastes.

As much as possible was preserved of the old structure. The moulding and embossing of the ceilings were carefully restored, the kaleidoscopic design of the floor was repaired, and the walls were painted pale yellow to give them a new, gentler character.

In order to furnish a space of such an outstanding architectural quality as this, just a few, very well chosen, pieces were used. In the living room, between the two French windows, stands a storage unit with glass shelves above. The seating consists of a black leather sofa, a classic Corbusier chaise longue, also in black leather, and an easy chair with red and grey upholstery. An original art nouveau coffee table has four enormous castors supporting a sheet of glass.

It takes very little to transform some spaces, like the hallway shown on the opposite page, into very pleasant places. The original floor tiles and window frames alone, of a quality hard to find these days, create a period ambience, which is then emphasized by the enormous ceramic jar and simple art nouveau seat.

Good restoration work, as in this case, must, above all, be respectful of the past. This apartment is full of beautiful elements that were well worth preserving.

The marvellous design of the original art nouveau ceramic floor is one of the major features of this room.

The hallway and corridor have also been very sympathetically restored.

Beneath the
waves

The dining-room is very simply
furnished to make the most of
the dramatic architectural space.

The ceiling of this house is divided into a succession of curving bare brick vaults, reminiscent of rolling waves, across the entire area. The spaces beneath are designed with simplicity and style, complementing the magnificent structures of the house and enhancing its stark beauty.

From the exterior, a long corridor leads into the spacious and sparsely furnished dining room, which is separated from the kitchen by sliding wood doors. Wood is also used on the floors throughout the entire house. The dining room furniture consists only of a long pale wood sideboard — next to which a huge pot has been placed — a glass-topped table on castors and four wicker chairs. A splendid sisal rug covers the floor. The kitchen is in pale wood; a counter is visible through its open door.

*The main corridor runs the
entire width of the house.*

The bedroom is welcoming and well balanced, decorated in pale, natural colours. In the centre, the large bed has an upholstered headboard, on either side of which are bedside tables cantilevered out from the wall. The wicker easy chair has a bright throw, matching the colours of the picture on the wall.

The angle-poise lamps on each side of the bed are a surprising detail, since they are more often used in an office or on a work desk. However, they are in fact very practical for reading in bed, as they allow greater mobility and choice of position for the light source. The ceiling is highlighted with a small spot high up on the wall.

Harmony dominates these interiors, to create a haven of all-pervading peace. Most of the colours are natural tones, very similar to each other in shade and tone, thus avoiding brusque contrasts and creating an especially relaxing decor.

At each end of the long corridor a glass door leads out into the garden.

The bedroom is warm and welcoming, with its natural tones and subdued lighting.

Two very up-to-date kitchens

This kitchen is spacious enough to accommodate a secondary dining room.

The two kitchens featured on these and the following pages incorporate several of the trends popular in current interior design, although each of them adapts modern features in its own way, with its own style and peculiarities.

The first is huge, with two cooking areas, two extractors and several sinks. The flooring is in discreet brown ceramic tiles that disguise stains and dirt. The walls are half clad in granite tiles, while the remainder is faced in fine yellow Venetian stucco. The kitchen units are aligned against three of the walls, leaving the fourth free. Most of the units are in a metallic dark blue-green finish, with a few paler blue shelves and trimming and a granite worktop. One end of the kitchen contains a pleasant dining area furnished with simple wooden chairs and table. The overall mood of the room is workmanlike, but also of stylish modernity.

The second kitchen and dining room are again in the same space, but are not totally united: they are independent spaces although no architectural barriers separate them. Again the flooring is in brown ceramic tile, but with salmon pink

The furniture chosen for this integrated dining room is slightly rustic.

Venetian stucco on the upper walls and wood panelling on the lower walls.

The duck egg blue kitchen units have wood worktops and are arranged along two of the walls, as well as being used to form a practical central island unit. The dining area here is on the far side of the space, where the walls are painted plain cream to mark this area's different function and independence.

Both kitchens are spacious and their logical layout facilitates ease of use. These are excellent spaces, not just for cooking and other household tasks but also to be enjoyed as alternative living rooms, just as family life in the past used to revolve around the kitchen and the fireplace. As homes became automated the kitchen became a clinical room for machines, but these two examples express a desire to reinstate them as the centre of the family's social life.

The dining area can be seen in the background.

The unusual colour scheme of duck egg blue and salmon pink gives this kitchen a very modern look.

Waking up to a patio

The term functionalism is often used to conceal a dictatorship that reduces design to its unacceptable minimums. Speculators in building and architecture have predetermined what rooms a house should have: living room, dining room, kitchen, bathroom and bedrooms (plus perhaps two or three optional spaces: study, utility room). Much of the value of a house in any particular location will depend on the size of these rooms and the number of bedrooms.

Many of domestic architecture's most attractive spaces were no longer built when experts failed to find a pragmatic use for them. Anyone who has a room with a name that has fallen into disuse – a tea room, gallery, observatory, cellar – or with no name at all is sitting on a treasure.

In this house is one such priceless privilege: a patio next to the bedroom. Here it is possible to lie in bed and watch the rays of the sun creep through the shutters on a Sunday morning; follow the shadows of the blinds as they move across the walls; linger over the newspaper with a cappuccino and croissant sitting on the patio; sunbathe in this winter sun trap. All absolutely dispensable activities, but who would not rather dispense with other things to be able to enjoy them?

There are several give-away signs that the original building is an old one: the masonry wall at the head of the bed, the hand-crafted door frames, the very high ceilings. The designers have made every effort to extend this aesthetic to the rest of the house. The materials, the furnishings and the fittings used in other rooms in the house, such as the recently-renovated kitchen and bathroom, echo images of days gone by. The bathroom has a basin fitted in a marble top, with a single gold tap, and the floor tiles are also used on the walls. In the kitchen, the cupboards have lattice doors and the old-style marble kitchen sink presents a strong contrast with the vitroceramic cooker hob; nostalgia meeting high-tech.

In the kitchen, the units have lattice-work doors that are modern but with a retro feel.

The bathroom vanity unit is reminiscent of a Victorian washstand.

The bedrooms are set around a sunny patio, and each one has large French windows opening into it.

Visual continuity

The long wall of this living-dining room holds a wooden storage unit and bookshelf that runs right over the structural pillars and out of the area, past the blue partition that marks the limit of the room, until it links with the corridor. It unifies the wall, hiding changes of level in the surface, but stops short of the ceiling to avoid appearing too heavy and making the room feel enclosed

The living area features a modern sofa upholstered partly in electric-blue and partly in blue and white striped cloth. The coffee table is a bold, contemporary model consisting of a single wood and stainless steel leg topped by a sheet of clear glass. On the far side is an angular armchair and matching footstool in tan leather. The light from the windows is controlled and filtered by translucent white Roman blinds, which can be adjusted to change the mood of the room.

The dining area, next to the bright blue partition, is outstandingly simple and discreet. It is furnished with a rectangular walnut table and walnut chairs with plain white upholstery. The lighting here is by spotlights on a track, which again can be adjusted to alter the mood.

All the interiors in this home are very well balanced, with each piece in its right place. Nevertheless, this balance appears to be absolutely natural – rather than being forced, rigid or imposed – the result of informality and everyday living.

The long storage unit runs right through the living and dining area, and out to the corridor.

Simple and stylish, each piece of furniture has been carefully chosen to match the mood of the room.

Warm orange

This living room, with its warm, orange-coloured light, contains objects collected from various sources and in the most diverse of styles. The designer has applied two parallel strategies: the use of one overall colour to give the room unity and a miscellany of interesting details to fill corners.

The room is elongated, with a skylight in the centre and French windows at one end, revealing a small patio garden with a tree, enclosed by a wall.

The stoneware floor tiles echo those used in traditional clay adobes. The walls are sponged in two tones of warm orange to break up the homogeneous surface and the same finish has been applied to the ceilings across the space.

The various sectors of the room are arranged in a series of interconnecting areas: study, library, dining room, living room and garden. This ensures that the various activities contained in this one room are clearly differentiated.

Almost all the furniture is classic in style, in dark-toned woods with a profusion of moulding. Background lighting is provided by small spotlights set in the ceiling, with table tamps set round the room to add mood lighting.

The owner's taste for the dramatic and unusual is illustrated by the statue of a reclining Buddha and the artistically disarranged table cloth set with a vase of lilies.

Changing levels

The warmth of bare brick visually dominates this interior.

The spaces in this majestic home have radically different ceiling levels, so they range from a stunning double-height living room at one end of the building, which leads into a series of narrow, elegant rooms after the ceiling height has dropped.

In the main living room, the gaze is drawn upwards by a full-height wall of beautiful, warm, terracotta-coloured bricks, which seems to stretch upwards into infinity. As seen from above, the layout of the living room is perfectly balanced, its central elements arranged in the form of a cross. A specially-designed, curvy, feminine, sofa stands with its back against the rather more masculine bare brick wall. A second, more conventional, sofa is next to it, also upholstered in white, with two red canvas chairs placed opposite. In the centre is a simple, modern glass and steel coffee table, but an iron stove with open flue pipe is the true focal point of this area.

The floor throughout is polished wood, but the seating sits on a large sisal rug.

Different areas are marked out with a series of rugs.

At one end of this room the ceiling height drops, forming a far more secluded room with a vaulted ceiling. The changes in level succeed each other smoothly and naturally, creating an astonishingly beautiful space.

The single-height space has been left practically empty, except for an unusual iron and glass side table, on and around which several artworks are displayed.

Balance, visual clarity and the unusual combination of volumes are the reigning qualities of this house, whose success lies in the fact that each space has been assigned a relative importance and then decorated accordingly.

A collection of modern artworks is arranged around an unusual glass and iron credenza.

The space under the vaulted ceiling has been left open and uncluttered.

Unusual structures

The structure of any house both gives it shape and limits its areas. How much space is available, the format of each room and the convenient or inconvenient corners of a house all depend on its structure. As an example, here is an interior in which columns, sloping ceilings and partitions create complicated settings.

Towards one end of this room there is a huge central partition, which acts as the visual link between two floors while at the same time separating areas and providing some privacy. This structure is painted in a cream similar to that of the false ceiling, both of which contrast with the reddish tone of the parquet. Behind the partition is a living room, of which the photograph shows only a yellow easy chair and a series of horizontal wall units.

The living room extends into a corridor, which is interrupted by two nib walls with a bookcase in between. At the far end, under a sloping ceiling, stands a large writing desk. Both desk and bookcase are made of the same wood that is used to clad some of the walls.

In this home, the architectural structures tend to occupy the visual foreground, since they are too strikingly original to be ignored. As a result, most of the furniture is built-in and discreet, harmonizing with its surroundings. However, some items have been treated like sculptures placed in the space: an aristocratic chair by Charles Rennie Mackintosh and an avant-garde armchair by Dutchman Gerrit Rietveld.

This large partition links two floors and separates the living room from the rest of the space.

The Mackintosh chair is treated almost like a carefully-placed sculpture.

Contained passion

A sharply sloping ceiling and an intense red are the factors setting the scene in this multi-purpose space: living room, studio, library.

One end is laid out for relaxation, with a bright-blue corner sofa in lively contrast to the rich, warm tone used for the walls and ceiling. The upholstery on the sofa is piped in red, and the cushions heaped casually on it are the same colour as the wall and piped in blue, to create a play of alternate colours. The walls around the sofa are hung with a selection of paintings of very different periods, styles and sizes. In front of the seating, the designer has placed a richly patterned blue and red Oriental rug, on which stands a modern glass coffee table on giant castors.

The sloping ceiling directly above the sofa is only just high enough for people to sit comfortably, so the designer has built a wooden-topped brick shelf to separate the sofa slightly from the wall and bring it out into a slightly higher space. The sloping roof also creates a psychological feeling of protection and tranquillity.

Views of the living area, under its sloping ceiling. The designer has based the colour scheme on the contrast between bright red and blue.

In a smaller space, using such a strong colour on both walls and ceiling could have seemed claustrophobic, but in this large area it works very well, creating a warm, cosy effect.

The centre of the room is occupied by a staircase leading downward. Around the opening in the floor is a barrier of simple glass panels, set between chrome-plated metal supports. The staircase itself has a plain tubular steel chrome-plated handrail. The use of clear glass panels without any framework for the barrier prevents it from visually interrupting the area of the room.

At this end of the room is the study area and library. The study has a large skylight flooding the space with natural light. The entire end wall is lined with one enormous bookcase, providing plenty of space for a library of books.

Downstairs there is a small dining room, curtained off from the main ground floor space and decorated in simple cream and natural wicker, in great contrast to the rich colours of the room above.

The floor is covered in parquet, with different levels to differentiate between the various uses of the space.

The standard lamp in the dining room bathes the entire space in a warm yellow light. Although the colour scheme is different from the living room upstairs, certain elements, such as the blue armchair and the maroon curtains, pick up the colours used there.

Empty space

In this stunning interior there is hardly any furniture and very few decorative objects, since they are unnecessary. The space is so impressive and the architectural features so innovative that items of furniture would act merely as visual obstacles.

The empty, bare double-height living room is overwhelmingly vast. Reminiscent of a gymnasium, its floor is completely covered with parquet and the walls have been left white. The ceiling, also in white, is pierced by a few long, narrow skylights that admit natural light. This great room doubles up as both living room and squash court.

At the far end, behind a sheltering glass partition, two floors can be seen linked by a light staircase, characterized by its slight curve, transparent sides and simple wooden handrail. The entrance to the house is on the lower floor, where the only pieces of furniture visible are a couple of modern metal chairs.

The floor above has a long, oval, glass-topped central table. Each of the two sides of the room features a semi-circular glazed space containing counters, one of which contains a sink and taps. This upper space also forms a viewing gallery from which to follow the game in the squash court/ living room below. These spaces are used for radically different functions that exist together in the same area, which make them particularly unusual.

A simple, gently curving staircase links the two floors.

Overall view of the full space.

An art nouveau palace

Mosaics, wallpaper, paintings and friezes decorate the walls of the corridor.

This splendid art nouveau home, with the city at its feet, is inspired by the mosaic fragments of the Park Güell and the undulating forms of the architecture of Gaudí. The interior spaces coexist in friendly harmony, both concealing and revealing the structure, drawing from it and enhancing its beauty. In the dining room, traditional Arabic mosaics cover most of the lower walls, combined with elaborate mouldings and original friezes. Moorish arches, set with circular stained glass panels, crown the tall, imposing windows and the area has a spectacular vaulted ceiling, also with a geometric Arabic design. An original art nouveau design has been used for the wallpaper. In the centre of the room is a stunning avant-garde table, surrounded with simple modern chairs to avoid taking attention from the art nouveau design.

The corridor has also retained original art nouveau elements and has been designed in harmony with them.

The dining room is set beneath a vaulted ceiling in a space of sumptuous architecture.

In another of the rooms a study has been installed, decorated with very up-to-date furniture. Its decor is an example of sobriety and deliberate restraint. The bathroom is clad in marble, with a slab of the same material holding the steel washbasin, a mirror and a sweet display stand, here used as storage.

The elaborate and exuberant interior of this home is full of beauty. The discreet furniture and accessories allow their setting to take the leading role. This would not have been possible with an imitative or kitsch decor; by using simple, modern furnishings, the fantastic architectural setting has been highlighted and enhanced.

The bathroom is the only place in the house that does not share the exuberant baroque art nouveau style.

Modern furniture has been chosen for the study in order to update the 19th-century atmosphere.

Serene reality

A serenity beyond fashions and fads reigns over this interior of white walls and gentle contrasts, in which furniture and decorative objects have been carefully arranged to create pleasant corners and clearly differentiated areas.

This square, well-proportioned living-dining room opens to the exterior through large, glazed sliding doors. Light reaches even the most unexpected corners, so that interior and exterior merge to create a single harmonious whole. In the living area large modern, items, such as the two sofas with their blue and white striped throws, visually offset the more gracefully classic pieces like the pair of tub chairs. The dining room has an unusual table, formed from a glass top set on two giant pots, and simple wood and canvas director chairs. At the far end, a built-in open staircase leads to the floors above, and a corridor opens onto the terrace outside.

The white walls contrast with the rustic, hard-wearing red tile floor and two kilim rugs provide attractive notes of colour.

This peaceful interior is characterized by a steady, calm rhythm. What might have been a rigid symmetry is broken by the pattern of the rugs, the casual throws and the natural shape of the indoor plants.

The resulting, calculated, disorder encourages a more relaxed, user-friendly enjoyment of the space. A chair can be moved, slippers left lying by the couch or a newspaper spread out on the table with no fear of upsetting a painstakingly staged arrangement.

General view of the serene living-dining room.

The glass dining table does not visually disrupt the space.

Making the most of corners

In the form of a narrow corridor, the space of this interior has been meticulously arranged to make full use of every square inch, while leaving the centre free to facilitate circulation and avoid crowding.

The long, straight room has doors at each end that open onto the exterior. The original, eye-catching ceiling consists of several brick vaults supported by sturdy concrete beams. The floor is covered in red terracotta tiles, which contrast nicely with the overall colour scheme of white and pale lilac. The gentle curves of the built-in staircase, with its wrought ironwork handrail and step details, and the curved front of fireplace add movement to an otherwise rather rigidly straight space.

The staircase separates two areas: the living room on one side and the kitchen on the other. The living room is arranged around the lilac fireplace: a comfortable printed fabric sofa with large cushions, a wicker coffee table, a wooden table with a large lamp, a Windsor chair and a built-in storage unit similar to the fireplace.

The kitchen is also the dining room. The cheerful red kitchen units are arranged in line, next to an old trunk and a display-case cupboard. Opposite, the dining area holds a light table with a wicker top and wrought-iron legs.

This interior is youthful, colourful and delicately naïve. Full use has been made of the space and architectural elements are used to divide the space.

The structural elements are the built-in staircase and fireplace.

At the far end, a glazed door leads out into the garden.

Living in the city

It is a well-known fact that the main problem with houses in cities is a lack of space. The high cost of urban land forces city-dwellers to squeeze as much as they can out of every square foot. On these pages are two bedrooms which overcome their rather small dimensions to produce a spacious overall effect.

The first stands on what once used to be a terrace. Aluminum and glass were used for the structure, then a wood parquet floor, rendered walls and a false ceiling were added. The final effect is very similar to any other bedroom in the house, but with far better natural lighting.

The width of the bedroom is taken up completely by the bed, so the designer has installed a continuous parquet platform as a base, which creates a change of level in the room. Besides the bed, the room holds only a table, a chair, a shelf and a series of cylindrical wooden hat boxes for storing the essential bedroom accoutrements. Clothes and all other accessories are kept in another room. These few elements are suitably arranged to create a comfortable environment. There are, of course, some obvious objections: the lack of space makes it rather difficult to get into bed, and it is always much more convenient to have a wardrobe inside the bedroom. However, the owners would not have been able to achieve this extra bedroom if they had insisted on these conditions.

While the means of getting round the lack of space in the second example are not identical, the two designs do share some very clear characteristics which help to illustrate the result of certain decisions.

A view of the bedroom from one end.

Using a platform as the base for the bed ruled out the use of the traditional bedside table, so a standard lamp for bedtime reading is placed to one side.

As in the first example, the bed is almost at floor level, in this case standing on a tatami (the plant-fibre surface traditionally used to cover floors in Japanese houses). This is not mere coincidence: a low bed occupies less space and visually creates a broader perception of the room.

To create a further feeling of space, there are no doors between the bedroom and the adjacent living room. While the existing stretch of wall allows a degree of independence between the two spaces, the two openings make the bedroom appear to be much bigger than it is.

This layout creates an interesting play of varying moods, which the designer has accentuated with an intelligent use of colour. The living room, painted in cold tones (blue, white and mauve), leads into a bedroom which is full of warm colours and welcoming light. The living room is a free and more open space, while the opposite effect is created in the bedroom, which exudes comfort and coziness.

The choice of a tatami as the base for the bed also rules out bedside tables. Here, lamps and bedtime reading are placed directly on the floor.

A view of the bedroom from the living room. The lilac-painted door in the background leads into the bathroom.

Good ideas

Good interior designs provide ideas that solve problems and satisfy needs. All the interiors of this cheerful, casual home are full of practical solutions and intelligent resources.

The living-dining room is arranged around a large terrace that can be used as a summer dining room. The sometimes dazzling light from outside is tempered by sturdy white roller blinds. The living room, of an elegance set somewhere between austerity and romanticism, is situated next to the glass doors that give onto the exterior. The main item of seating is the large white sofa, which has two bookcases behind. These bookcases do not reach the ceiling, so enough space was left above to create a display shelf on which several ceramic pieces stand and below this, echoing its shape, the lower shelf of the bookcase continues along the wall to act as a desk. In the centre, opposite the sofa, a coffee table stands on a sisal rug.

On the terrace an enchanting summer dining room has been created.

From the side of the bookcase, a shelf is continued along the wall to act as a desk.

The dining room stands beside a wood partition that encloses another room. On one side there are shelves to display a collection of urns, with an acid-etched glass door that slides across on rails to conceal this display area. The dining room itself has a simple glass table and iron chairs with pale grey upholstery, sitting on a modern rug.

The design of a room, apart from embellishing the space, should also increase the owners' comfort. The idea of beauty is completely subjective, and is frequently just the result of a sensation of comfort. This house offers numerous attractive ideas that are also very practical solutions to specific problems.

The display shelf continues round one end of the room, forming a kind of cornice that is also used to display the owners' collection of ceramic pots.

View of the dining room, with the display space for urns and its sliding screen.

In pink and blue

T hanks to their predominant colours, these two rather ordinary interiors have been transformed. Pink, in one case, and sky blue in the other have endowed complicated, almost empty spaces with originality and life.

Pink enlivens the corridors and the circulation space in this barn-like dwelling, pulling several disparate areas into one cohesive whole. One of the walls has also been faced with fine timber boards, and the tall glazed door to the exterior is also

in natural wood. The grey ceramic tile floor combines very well with the pale pink of the walls. At the far end, the steps of the staircase are painted grey, so that they seem to be a continuation of the floor.

The second interior is a bathroom tiled all round with sky-blue mosaic. The corner in the photograph contains the essential, very well balanced, elements. The white of the sanitary ware and the natural pale colour of the wood set off the blue of the mosaics perfectly.

Thanks to the use of one, cohesive colour to hold the scheme together, these interiors have been transformed into youthful, fresh, cheerful and casual spaces.

The bathroom, clad in sky blue mosaic, has been decorated with only a few simple pieces in pale natural wood.

Colour brings together several interconnected spaces, making them one.

Well
defined

These two totally different interiors do have something in common: their strong, well-defined lines, their balanced spaces and their simple colour combinations. All is perfection; there are no discordant notes. They are environments designed to be lived in, full of vitality and far away from the cold decor of catalogues and decoration manuals.

The photograph on the opposite page shows a two-storey home in which the open wooden staircase captures almost all the attention. The ground floor, with its terracotta flooring, contains a simple,

bright dining room located opposite large glazed doors; a passage area with a hall table and a brightly colored Oriental rug; and a bright, cheerful kitchen which is out of sight, round the corner. All the rooms on the floor above are hidden behind a wood partition, so only the landing is visible. Everywhere are simple shapes, in natural materials and soft colours harmonizing together to create the whole.

The bathroom follows some of the most revolutionary design trends. Two stainless steel washbasins with piping in full view are half sunk into a marble ledge. The long,

elegant, polished metal water spouts match the accessories that adorn the room, and a large mirror visually duplicates the space. The wall is clad in glazed white mosaic with, at the top almost touching the ceiling, a discreet border. The smaller the space, the more meticulous the design called for. All the elements placed in this bathroom have been reduced to their bare minimum; the basis of the decoration is quality materials and simplicity of form.

The bathroom is the product of avant-garde design trends.

Simple shapes and soft, natural colours create an elegant interior.

A vital decor

Some interiors are visually relaxing; they are serene spaces that calm emotions and temper the senses. By contrast, the vital decor of this house animates the spirit.

One of the main spaces is the study, which has a false ceiling of strips of plastic. The walls are clad in ochre Venetian stucco, while the flooring is black, shining marble.

At the far end, a crammed bookcase runs the full length of one wall, while the desk chair is a classic French piece with floral upholstery. Natural light enters through glazed doors that open onto the exterior.

The most cheerful room is the brightly-coloured kitchen. The kitchen units, arranged in a 'U' shape, are a combination of warm natural wood and yellow lacquer.

The patterned upholstery of the easy chair, the armchair and the original winged table all combine to create a youthful environment.

The Venetian stucco enlivens the study walls with fresh colour.

The walls are painted yellow, with the area behind the worktop covered with tiles in shining bottle-green; the same colour enlivens the floor. An oval table emerges from the units to rest on a strong steel leg.

In the totally mosaic-clad bathroom, the bathtub is partially concealed behind a partition and the ceramic washbasin is sunk into a wall-to-wall vanity unit.

The occasional discreet touch of colour, an original piece of furniture here and there, an eye-catching print, any detail – however simple it may be – can enliven an environment and transform it into a unique space.

The bathtub is concealed behind a partial partition.

A table emerges from the kitchen units and rests on a single steel leg.

Minimal expression

The elements that go to make up this house are very few – only the absolute essentials. They are very precisely placed, creating environments of charismatic perfection.

The different pieces of furniture are framed by Mediterranean-style arches, sinuous and painted white to blur and soften their outlines. In a small space, behind a large door with rounded corners, is a pleasant living room, caressed by the bright light that enters through a glazed door. The area is characterized by a very unusual, exotic, avant-garde quality that has been created by a combination of colonial-style pieces, such as the large wicker sofa, and others more modern in design, for example the coffee table with castors and small drawers. There is an audacious chair with a leopard-skin print back that matches the table lamp and the cushion. Everything is arranged on a sisal rug.

In the hallway, beside the white staircase, with its tiled steps and wooden trim, there is an elegant, solitary iron chair and, at its side, a shining sphere that stands alone against an immaculate white background.

A chair and a black sphere are the only pieces in the hallway.

The small living room is very exotic.

Brought up to date

This home has been decorated with antique, valuable and perfectly restored pieces. Nevertheless, the ambience that has been created is neither classic nor traditional. The antique pieces, possibly handed down through the family, are combined with modern, youthful items, giving rise to rooms of great personality, style and beauty.

The living and dining rooms, in which most of the social life of the house takes place, have floors of large rectangular tiles. The living room, the ceiling of which features a number of recessed lights, is full of vitality and elegantly, though casually, furnished. The seating consists of two checked upholstery sofas around a simple glass-topped table. At the far end there is

a second seating area with two period easy chairs upholstered in electric blue, and a wooden coffee table. The most unusual piece, however, is the antique wooden filing cabinet in the background.

The outstanding elements in this living room are the two period easy chairs and the antique filing cabinet.

General view of the two seating areas in the living room.

The kitchen is cheerfully colourful and bright, with vivid yellow walls. Small antique country-style cupboards stand harmoniously side-by-side with modern kitchen units.

In the master bedroom, painted in the same colours as the living-dining room, the furniture is arranged as in a hotel suite; there is a bed and a small seating area.

When decorating a house with antique furniture, it is not necessary to restrict oneself to a classic style of design. In this case, the period pieces have been beautifully integrated into youthful, fresh interiors.

The kitchen is bright and colourful.

The bedroom has a small seating area in the window, so it also acts as a small personal living space.

The house of the future

Incredible architectural structures form this original, innovative and daring home. Its interiors are as striking as the exterior and the furniture and decor seem to disappear in the midst of peculiar, complicated forms.

Columns, pillars, cornices and large glazed walls have taken possession of the house, creating dramatically empty, powerful spaces of irregular outline. One of the façades is totally of glass, giving the building the appearance of a glass box since the interior can be seen through it – a white interior in which only a picture, the dramatic curve of a staircase and a curious modern chair break the solitude.

The walls are white and the floor is paved in marble of the same colour. The area is washed with bright light from concealed sources and the stark shapes are reflected in the still water of the pools outside.

The totally glazed facade, running round a small garden.

The curious modern chair stands out as the only piece of furniture.

The bedroom furniture consists merely of a large double bed and a couple of simple bedside tables, one of which holds a small orange lamp. The most striking element in this room is the structure of the beams that decorate the ceiling.

Houses like this one, with such bold and revolutionary architecture, must be decorated with care, since any form of excess, however small or insignificant, could upset the aesthetic balance.

The bedroom is dominated by its beam structure.

Inside, a dramatic interplay of light and shade is created.

The heart of the house

This is a room that surely invites sociability, in which long hours will be spent reading, conversing and devoted to social and family life. It is a comfortable space, in which nothing is superfluous or in the way: everything responds to specific needs.

Next to the staircase leading to the floors above, the big, rectangular living room is dominated by pale natural wood – the parquet floor, the stair and its handrails, the door leading to the kitchen. At one end of the room a pleasant dining area has been created, consisting of a square extendible table and a set of woven wicker chairs. A simple sideboard stands against the wall. In a corner next to the stair stand a bar and a drinks trolley.

Presiding over the other end of the room is an open fireplace, with large, built-in bookcases on either side of the chimney breast. Arranged around the bookcase is an exceptionally welcoming and homely living area. The seating arrangement consists of a comfortable white sofa, an easy chair in the same colour and a rocking chair. In the centre, three small tables are arranged at right angles.

Once the main pieces of furniture have been chosen, attention must be paid to the accessories, to the decor, to all those details that make a home one's own. Here, the paintings, the candles in the fireplace and the cushions add a personal touch.

The dining room, with its extending table, is situated beneath the staircase.

The living room is simple, stylish and inviting.

The plant kingdom

The most significant aspect of these two rooms is the extensive use of wicker and cane, which cover walls and floors as well as being used for some of the furniture. It adds its own particular touch of nature to these elegant spaces, transforming them into very casual and youthful areas.

The living room is regular and well-proportioned, totally surrounded by large, multi-paned glazed doors. The sloping false ceiling is entirely covered with strips of cane, while the floor has a sisal carpet. Yellow curtains hang at the green-framed windows, filtering the strong sunlight. The seating consists of two large, upholstered cream sofas, both with a wide, blue and gold striped throw, and two wicker chairs. The centre of the room has been left practically empty, except for a number of coffee tables dotted round the space. Behind one of the sofas is a simple dining area with a rectangular folding table and three garden chairs.

The bedroom also has glazed doors giving onto the terrace; the curtains and the floor are identical to those of the living room. The large, elegant double bed features a rounded headboard and romantic, white, frilled bed linen. At its side stands a classic bedside table.

Unity is something fundamental in a home. However different the rooms in it may be, they should all reveal the same spirit and maintain an overall personality.

Behind one of the sofas a simple dining area has been created.

The bedroom follows the same decorative style as the living room.

With its cane ceiling, sisal carpet and wicker chairs, this room has an abundance of natural materials

A fairy tale

Colours, lights and curious shapes are given free rein in this original interior, to create an ensemble of magical beauty in which everything seems possible. The modern furniture acquires new meaning, while conventional furniture is seen from a new, daring perspective.

The discreet pale yellow walls soften the visual impact of a highly varied ensemble, thus preventing one's gaze from becoming lost among so many colours. But this is where the discretion ends: all the rest is exuberance and daring. The large sofa has bold upholstery with large blue and yellow squares that cover the seat, backrest and armrests. The masculine personality of this contrasts with a curvy, feminine easy chair upholstered in bright red on the far side. In the centre, the moveable glass-topped coffee table on castors is both attractive and very practical, as are the very unusual modern side tables

The dining room is in a corner, between two columns and set under a large window with translucent Roman blinds. The simple round table rests on just one single, slim leg that is attached to the floor. Around it are arranged four timber-frame chairs, each in the same fabric but in a different colourway.

One's first impression on contemplating this interior is of a cheerful space full of vitality, suggesting that the owners of the house are young, carefree, fun-loving people who like to experiment and want nothing to do with conventionality.

The simple yellow walls discreetly soften the visual impact of the wide variety of colours used elsewhere in the room.

The dining room is lit with a modern metal space frame lighting system

A summer dining area

During the warm summer months, life in the open air becomes a necessity. Gardens, neglected through winter, are recovered, open galleries refurbished and balconies and patios exploited to the full. Such is the case of the terrace featured here.

The terrace crowns an urban block in the centre of a bustling city. At one time it was impossible to relax in this part of the house, but a latticework screen placed all around the area gave it some privacy: now vines climb mischievously up the lattice from sober brick planters.

In order to create an effect of warm homeliness, two vivid Oriental rugs that perfectly match the terracotta tiling have been spread out on the floor. The seating arrangement consists of an elegant wood garden bench with a matching arm chair; the centre table is a circular wooden one with a sturdy turned pillar and three splayed feet; a few small urns and a metal watering can are artfully placed.

The decoration of a terrace must follow the same rules as that of an interior. The objective is to achieve a welcoming area that is full of life, and all resources are valid to attain this end.

A trellis provides the terrace with privacy and isolates it from the outside world.

The Oriental rug immediately gives the terrace the feeling of being a room outside.

Country style brought up to date

The traditional rustic style goes back to days gone by, when everyone lived in close contact with nature, and when the house - the home - was unchanging in the face of passing years, a guardian and a protector of values, customs and memories. But times change, and now we live in a period of constant transformations and trials. This rustic and welcoming house therefore breaks with tradition and adapts its country style to present-day tastes.

As a general rule, kitchens are the living heart of country houses: they are warm and welcoming spaces, designed for family life, and the kitchen illustrated below is no exception. Its thick walls and curved ceiling enclose a colourful room, full of vitality. The furniture is ranged along one of the walls, leaving the centre free for a dining table. Instead of everything being hidden away in cupboards, it is all on show and to hand - now just as a display feature, but originally because this kind of room would have been in constant use.

The landing is an explosion of vivid colour, with its yellow and burnt-orange walls, green-framed windows and deep green and white striped table cloth and matching cushion covers.

Full of homely clutter, the kitchen looks as if it is in constant use.

The rich colours of the landing present a wonderful colour contrast.

A peaceful refuge

Although combined with white, with natural wood and with the earthy tones of the floor tiles and mosaic, it is blue which reigns supreme in every corner of this bedroom and its adjoining bathroom: walls, ceiling, bed linen and upholstery. It really is fascinating to see how the extensive use of a single colour affects the perception of a space, quite independently of questions of taste and sensibility; here is a particularly intense and lovely colour: the colour of the skies of the Matisse cut-outs, of Jujol's ceilings and, in its most concentrated version, of the monochrome Yves Klein canvases. It is first used to establish associations between normally unrelated, disparate elements; then a dialogue has been created, a play on similarities and contrasts which is somehow much more in keeping with the arts than with the interior of a room.

Details of the bedroom and its associated bathroom. The blue colour used throughout brings together a collection of disparate elements into a cohesive whole.

Touches of colour

The items that decorate these interiors are cheerful, original and entertaining. Their design is picturesque and the daring form of the odd piece conceals intelligent solutions, conceived to solve problems of space. To all this is added enchanting touches of vivid colour.

One of the rooms featured here is a youthful, carefree dining area. The main item is a large, multi-coloured piece of furniture that acts as a dividing panel, behind which a small study is hidden. It consists of different drawers and boxes of odd dimensions and contrasting colours, set over a harlequinade base that joins up with the high skirting band. The remarkable table consists of four coloured legs - two brown and two yellow - on which two superimposed glass sheets rest. The chairs are also unusual, with their undulating backrests and seats and different coloured legs.

On the facing page is the enchanting bathroom, with its striking apple green walls. The washbasin is a modern design in polished stainless steel, with the plumbing featured in full view.

The overall ambience of this room is of a fun atmosphere, with its bright colours and interesting shapes.

The walls of the bathroom are decorated with simple, child-like drawings.

Zone of passage

Two wings of the same dwelling are joined by a long corridor, which links both parts with such elegance that it acquires value in its own right, its own personality - a unique, differentiating character not often found in circulation space. The success of this arrangement lies in the fact that care has been lavished on even the tiniest detail, and this corridor has been considered as a fundamental part of the house.

A wall of glass sheets, fitted closely together without any framing, creates a reality that is part magical, part summery, the main attraction of which is its visual simplicity. The corridor is lit by discreet recessed lights in the ceiling. A translucent sliding glass door separates it from the rest of the interior, acting as a visual barrier.

The entire dwelling is characterized by roomy, open interiors and abundant natural light. The interior of the corridor features pale wood parquet flooring that makes the most of the light entering through the glass wall. Next to this wall, a simple, modern wooden bench that is both seat and table offsets the predominant emptiness.

The materials – glass sheets and blocks, wood – used to build and shape this home are all very modern and have been used to create elegant environments that demand the simplest of decors.

Running parallel with the corridor is a covered cloister, open on one side.

The bench is used as both seat and table.

Experimental decoration

Design, like art, must be prepared to innovate, to incorporate new, unusual pieces - in short, it must experiment with available resources to modify and re-interpret reality. In this interior, apparently incompatible elements have been successfully combined, and fantastic, revolutionary structures created.

The key space in this ultra-modern home is a large room split into two areas: living room and kitchen. The living room is arranged beneath a false slatted ceiling linked to another, more conventional, white ceiling over the kitchen area. Across the full length of the space is a huge, wooden bookcase, which contains a large number of disks and CDs. In the centre of this structure is an arched area containing a writing desk with a portable computer.

The living room furniture is arranged asymmetrically around two windows. Between them, a rectangular mirror seems to have been deliberately placed to upset the balance.

In the centre of the room, a large metal sink in an island unit indicates the start of the kitchen area. The worktops and the units themselves are brushed stainless steel, creating a modern, industrial feel in direct contrast to the comfortable softness of the living space behind.

The living room in the background and the kitchen in the foreground are at once both joined and separated.

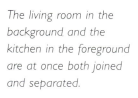

The writing desk looks towards the kitchen area.

The cold, almost icily, elegant bathroom is pure design. It is totally enveloped in translucent blue glass, with discreet recessed lights in the ceiling providing tempered, relaxing light. At the far end, a vertical sheet of glass conceals the toilet behind. The wooden bath is surprisingly warm in such a cold setting. The loft reveals the house's final surprise - a magnificent roof observatory.

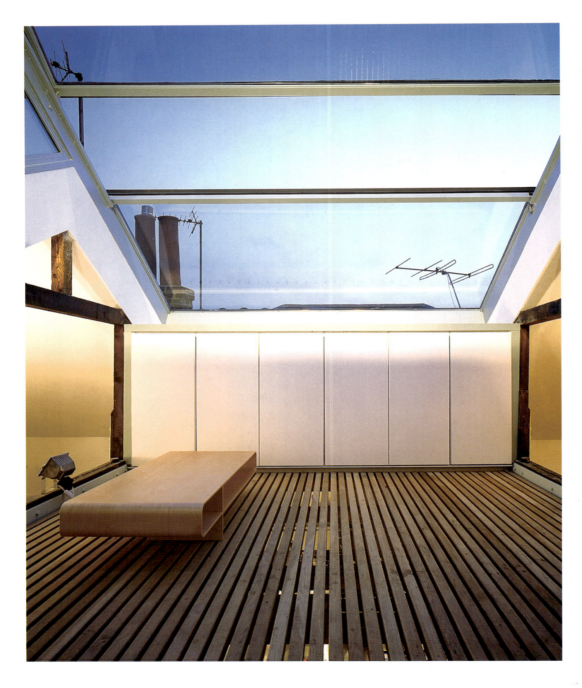

A modern observatory has been created in the gable roof.

The bathroom walls are of blue translucent glass.